Celebrate Life After 50

CELEBRATE

Life After 50

Roger Palms

VICTOR BOOKS

A DIVISION OF SCRIPTURE PRESS PUBLICATIONS INC.
USA CANADA ENGLAND

Unless otherwise noted, Scripture
quotations are from the *Holy Bible,
New International Version*®. Copyright
© 1973, 1978, 1984 by International Bible
Society. Used by permission of Zondervan Publishing
House. All rights reserved. Other quotations are from
the *Authorized (King James) Version of the Bible* (KJV).

Editors: Carole Streeter and Barbara Williams

Designer: Andrea Boven
Cover Photo: Laurance B. Aiuppy, FPG International

**Library of Congress
Cataloging-in-Publication Data**

Palms, Roger C.
    Celebrate life after 50 / Roger C. Palms
        p. cm.
    ISBN 1-56476-453-2
    1. Middle aged persons—Religious life. 2. Christian life.
3. Lay ministry. 4. Vocation—Christianity. I. Title.
BV4579.5.P35   1995
248.8'5—dc20   95-41899
                                                            CIP

---

1 2 3 4 5 6 7 8 9 10 Printing/Year 99 98 97 96 95

Contents

1 Am I There Yet? **7**

2 Freedom to Be **23**

3 I'm Still Climbing **39**

4 Pupil, Teacher—Now I'm Both **57**

5 Come Snuggle with Me **81**

6 A Friend to My Children **103**

7 At Last I'm a Grandfather **121**

8 Together Is Good; Alone Is Good Too **135**

9 Never Stop Growing **151**

10 My Heritage, My Roots **169**

11 A Going-Away Party **187**

12 Death Plus Five Years **203**

Endnotes **221**

Am I There Yet?

1

"God never put anyone in a place too small to grow in."
Henrietta Cornelia Mears

"Live your life and forget your age."
Frank Bering

Louie Palermo is grinning. "I'm seventy-nine years old and I'm having a wonderful time." For years Louie traveled with his brother Phil as a music team with Youth for Christ. They were known as "The Apostles of Cheer." Louie, who is "retired," is still an apostle of cheer. With his mandolin, jokes, and a clear witness to Christ, he daily visits children's hospitals, veterans' hospitals, and community hospitals—as a bringer of joy to people who hurt. "I can't wait to get started when I wake up in the morning," he says. "Five years ago I had six-way bypass surgery. I know what people in the hospitals are going through. I can encourage them. I can help them."

Peter Enns in British Columbia is retired too. "But," he explains, "my philosophy is that there is more to life than sitting on a beach. I don't want to be one of those people who lie around doing nothing. There are just too many opportunities for ministry. I think, 'If you are still in good health and have a lot of energy, why not utilize it rather than spending your time being bored?'

"We were just invited to go to Russia for six months to work in Christian camps. The camping ministry there has mushroomed and they need extra help. I have retired friends who are building a Christian college in Lithuania, and an invitation has come for my wife and me to move there. The Lord willing, I will become interim president of Lithuania Christian College, a one-year assignment.

"As a Christian, I have a responsibility to use my time and energy in creative ways and to look for ministry opportunities. I never know what's around the next corner."

Now That My Hair Is Almost Gone

Opportunities for ministry are everywhere—opportunities to grow, to enjoy, to bring good to others, to be a mentor, a teacher, a friend. Yet there are still people who are missing out on this. They are older, but they won't admit it. They say, "Old? I'm not old." Or, they go the other direction and lament, "I'm too old to do anything." And they give up. They are old before their time. Still others have only one thought in mind, "I'm going to spend my retirement doing only what I want to do. I've worked hard; now it's time to enjoy myself." Yet, most of these people aren't enjoying themselves at all. They have no purpose and they know it.

We notice the man who says, "I'm not old," because he is usually trying hard to convince himself that he's still young. What the younger men are wearing, he tries to wear. His hours in the health club and the tanning salon aren't for health, but for image. He wants to be what he once was—lean and chiseled. And when his hairdresser suggests a toupee, he is ready. Before long, even his wife begins to look old to him.

With increasing numbers of older people, the battle is on to look young, to fight the inevitable. And with that battle may come a denial of reality that can turn into a denial of one of God's greatest blessings—maturity in the length of years.

There's the woman in her eighties who has convinced herself that she still turns the heads of young men. Recently, when she became ill, she refused medicine that might have the side effect of hair loss. She fills her conversation with talk of parties and young people who find her to be "so much fun."

Yet another person the same age says, "I'm old," which means, "I can't." So he doesn't do anything and won't be encouraged to try. His world becomes smaller and smaller until he alone is the center of his concentration. He expects aches and pains, and he feels them. He expects others to look after him, and they do. He is announcing loud and clear, "Watch out. Someday you'll be old and useless too."

And the person who says, "I'm retired; I don't intend to do anything but enjoy myself," has chosen to resign from what God can do with an individual in the later years.

There are opportunities as never before to invest the best years of our lives in fruitful and rewarding ministries. Generations coming along are looking for models, examples of what it means to grow older in the grace of God. Many retirees from their late fifties to their nineties know something that others have yet to discover—that God often saves the best for last.

But when those who are older pretend that they are not old, or do admit their age but assume that means quitting, or only want to live for themselves and play, everyone loses. Who will be the mentors, the examples, for the millions who know they will someday be older too? Who will offer direction? Who will show that God meant it when He said, "Even to your old age and gray hairs I am he, I am he who will sustain you"? (Isaiah 46:4)

If we have already decided that God doesn't want to use us anymore, we forsake what He is currently shaping us to be for His purpose, for our good, and for the good of others. Whether we deny aging, give in to it in surrender and resignation, or spend our energies only on ourselves, we may be missing out now on what can be our best years. No one should miss those opportunities. No one has to.

The Most Rewarding Time of Our Lives

God gives us life to invest in others. And if He also gives us freedom from a heavy schedule of work, He is offering us the opportunity for what could be the most rewarding years of our lives.

Carlton Carter of Scarborough, Ontario says, "I think you get a lot of fulfillment and satisfaction when you're involved in Christian ministry. God wants me to do more with my life in retirement than sit on a beach or be on a golf course. I'm in good health, and I believe one of the reasons I am is that I'm active and using my mind. I'm involved with people.

"I get a lot more kick out of life when I'm doing something worthwhile. There is a fallacy in the American dream that when you retire you go around pleasing yourself all the time. When you do that, I don't think you get the same satisfaction as when you're trying to accomplish something for the Lord."

Carter has been a teacher, principal, and area superintendent of schools. Since his retirement, he has been working with The Salvation Army as the administrator of their day-care program and the Christian Education Committee of his Corps. He says, "One of our projects is to prepare young adults for ministry by creating a Leadership Development Course. We have seventy people enrolled. Over forty of them are in their twenties and thirties. We're trying to motivate them to see the value of taking responsibility in the church.

"I'm taking this course too, and I lead a home Bible study group. Every person should continue learning throughout his lifetime. I'm continually learning."

Gwynn Lewis, Executive Director of The Sowers International, finds the contribution older people can make to ministry exciting. He says, "In a lot of countries outside North America, gray hair means something.

"I say, give God a year, even a few months. Go help in a missionary office. Keep the books to free up a missionary who is doing office work when he or she has the language, knows the culture, and could be out working among the people. You don't need the language; you're freeing up someone who has it.

"Retired pastors can do seminars for missionaries. They can almost pick their subject. Then they can also preach on weekends. In many places English is used at the Bible institutes; but even if it isn't, so many students want to use their English that they will translate for you.

"Retired farmers can teach animal husbandry or work with people on their farms, giving opportunities for evangelism. Or, people with craft skills can be part of a construction project.

"The cost is little. You can stay in homes. And even if your plane fare is too much, your church will probably help you. There are so many projects."

When Ritchie Allan of Ontario retired from the Royal Canadian Mounted Police as an assistant commissioner, he didn't sit around long.

"At retirement I assumed the position of church administrator in our Ottawa church for a few months while traveling periodically to Regina, Saskatchewan to provide management consulting services to Canadian Bible College/Canadian Theological Seminary. The following summer I took the position of vice president for administration at the college for four years. After that, I was assistant to the president for a year.

"In retirement I've had eighteen years of ministry, almost a second career. It has been great! And at age seventy-four, I look forward, Lord willing, to continue until it is time to meet Him personally.

"I know many people with tremendous gifts who retire early, but they haven't been encouraged to go into ministry. There are unlimited things they can do and teach."

Retired? What For?

To whom can young women turn when problems seem overwhelming, whether a career decision or abuse or questions of love? Who can give perspective? Not us if we refuse to be time-balanced persons whom God wants to provide to those who are younger. A wise and beautiful sixty-year-old or eighty-year-old is attractive and has much to offer to others.

Eva Prior is seventy-three years old and legally blind. She can't drive or read or watch television and, she says impishly, "I can't even see my own face in the mirror. But that might be a blessing in disguise!"

That doesn't stop her. She says, "I thank God that I was able to be in Bible Study Fellowship for five years and complete an in-depth study of His Word. The last year and a half of that course I was unable to see, but I have been able to get the lessons on tape. This study has given me a grounding in God's Word which I am able to share with others.

"Even with this difficulty, the Lord has not laid me aside. I have had the wonderful joy of discipling new Christians and sometimes older Christians who have been on the way for a long time but are struggling. They come to my home for discipling. It has been a wonderful joy to me because they're all ages and from different walks of life. God has brought them to me. I do believe that this has been even a greater blessing to me than to them."

Can a young man gain perspective on his own life without older men to help him? I know a man in his nineties who continues to mentor others. He does so by keeping abreast of what is happening in the world and advising those with less experience. He doesn't dominate or dictate. Rather, he listens, counsels, and from his perspective of years in the Scriptures and with the assurance that God will "never leave you or forsake you," is able to give credibility to what he says because he has proven it in his own life. He has experienced God over the long haul.

What if he refused to admit that he is ninety? What if

he either pretended to be younger (making himself un-appealing because he would appear to be foolish) or just hid away, assuming that he had done his part, had made his contribution, and was now too old? But he under-stands who he is and what he has to offer. This man continues to be an effective Christian advisor, effective because he has been where younger men are and knows that they need what he has to offer. They know it too.

Because he has the credentials, he is a magnet to men who find their way to his door. He has a ministry that will continue as long as God gives him physical strength and mental ability.

Who Will Help Them?

According to evangelist Howard Jones and other teach-ers, one of the great influences in the black family in years past was the extended group of older men and women who would discipline, teach, encourage, listen, and show from the experience of their years who God is and what He expects of younger people. Now this is changing, as fewer mature people are willing to accept the opportunity to be teachers and mentors to the fam-ily, the community, or the church.

What a contrast between those who do not admit to who they are (and to what they have to offer) and so become unavailable as mentors, and those who do admit to who they are, do make themselves available, and pass on to those coming behind them valuable helps for liv-ing.

Aging baby boomers are making midlife assessments. Busters are questioning what the boomers have left them. The unnamed X generation behind the busters is seeking for answers in a world that is confusing. There are value shifts going on around us. People speak of a spiritual quest, a search for meaningful faith. But, as they look around, who will help them with their search? Since there is very little Christian teaching within our culture, older, stable Christians have a teaching opportunity that is desperately needed.

We can be light-givers and hope-bringers to the generations behind us. We can use our abilities and resources for the benefit of others. And, when we do lose our health or our resources dwindle, we can still be attractive to those who need someone to talk to or pray with. We can be guides, counting each day of extended life as an opportunity to help someone along the road to a better life—in fact, to life itself through the One who is the way, the truth, and the life.

Old? What's That?

Will I be the missionary, the teacher, the servant God has enabled me to be? Or will I start to believe that I am "over the hill"?

If I tend to believe the media and the advertisers, I will give up. Young people are the models for what is exciting and desirable. Old is, well, old. Yet, ever so slowly even advertisers are becoming aware that certain "known facts" about older people are not true.

"Lost muscle ability can't be restored and improved"—but it can. "The heart pumps less as it ages"—not so, according to experts. "The mind goes." Barring illness, for many people it doesn't. In fact, older people can be stimulated intellectually and remain clear thinkers as long as they live.

I have a friend who runs marathons. Each time he sees runners in their seventies and eighties. They usually finish and usually win the race in their age class. Why? Because most of them are the only ones in their age class still running. Others have thought, "I'm too old."

Our newspaper ran a story about a man named Tom Lane. In 1915 he was on the University of Minnesota swim team. Today he's still swimming. When he enters a race, he says, "I get the gold medal every time." Why? Because he's the only one in his class. He's still free enough to be what he wants to be—a good swimmer—and age hasn't stopped him. Neither has something else—he's blind. His only problem in swimming is staying in his lane. Recently he has taken up two new sports, discus throwing and javelin.[1]

One "granny" tried to market an exercise video for her age group. She tried sixty-nine companies only to hear, "We don't target that age group." Why? They were convinced that what they'd heard about older people was true. According to *American Demographics*, the woman sold her exercise video herself—and it has already gone over one million in sales.

If I deny *what* I am, I also deny *who* I am. Age, and the experience that goes with it, is part of my identity. To deny my own identity is also to deny what God is still creating me to be. It is a denial of what I have been given by God to give away to others.

The need for older mentors goes beyond the family and community. Some of the key board members of Christian organizations are business people who decided not to hang on to their previous corporate careers. Instead, they have chosen retirement in order to become mentors, teachers, wisdom-givers in expanding ministries around the world. They are serving in evangelism, missions, and the local church.

The dean of a Christian college said recently that although some Christian ministries have wisely hired good business managers, many other Christian organizations lack wise business leadership at the top. He said, "I can name several organizations that are having difficulties because they need some experienced leadership in their business offices."

They need partners. A Christian business leader said, "There is a need for people with years of business experience who come out of the corporate world to give, to help, to free others, to offer support and strength. They can be servants, bringing to these many fine Christian ministries good business procedures and helping to implement them, so that those who are called to a ministry with people can continue to do it."

An army going into battle needs support personnel behind the lines. We have many who are equipped and eager to march out for Christ. Older Christians "behind the lines" can enable them, serving as capable support people and teachers.

So Many Are Ready

We mustn't ignore the extraordinary harvest going on in the world. In many places people are turning to Christ in great numbers. Often that openness comes suddenly and may not last a long time. National Christians are eager to accept help in bringing in the harvest and nurturing new believers while there is time. As older Christians, we can be their helpers.

Recently I was in Essen, Germany with the Billy Graham Mission. One day at lunch I was visiting with an interpreter from Poland and another from Greenland. I said, "Someday I'd like to teach in a Bible school in Africa or Latin America. Because the Gospel is spreading so fast there, the new Christians need teachers to help ground them in God's Word."

Immediately my two lunch companions responded, "Come help us. We need your help right now." The man from Poland spoke of Bible schools opening in his country but still needing teachers. "We want you to come help us," he said. The man from Greenland also pressed me, "Most of the people of Greenland live along the coast. Our Bible school operates from a ship. We travel from place to place and stay for a period of time operating our Bible school on the ship and then move on to the next location. Will you come and help us? Will you teach for us?"

I came away from that visit thinking, "My vision is too small. The need is everywhere."

Those who are retired and able to pay their own expenses can be invaluable in aiding mission agencies. Many pastors have listings and know of the needs or can point older Christians to agencies that will help them find the most needy places to serve.

In the monograph *Partners in the Gospel*[2] are these words: "In the past, windows of ministry opportunity may have emerged once every few centuries. Today they are opening up at a rate of three or four per year."

God has many mature believers who are ready to help the people who have only just come to faith. That this harvest in the world is happening at the same time that so many mature Christians are available to help them is, in the economy of God, no accident. Surely God knows how to bring the two together. The great harvest of new believers and the great number of mature believers are ready at the same time. Praying, dedicated, and willing workers will find their mission. There is a more powerful army of believers ready than most of us know. That army can and should include you and me.

Recently a corporate president said, "I'd retire now if I could give my time to teaching. My wife wants me to do it. She says I have a lot to offer."

Inner-city ministries and missions, as well as international missions, need such people to bring good skills and loving wisdom. God has given to the body such a variety of gifts. We who are older have had years to define and sharpen our gifts. Now, perhaps more than ever before, we can benefit the many ministries of the church!

Our Phase-Three Ministry

To agree with God that we are experienced and blessed helps us enter into a wonderful phase-three ministry of life. If the first phase of life was taken up with growth and education, and the second phase of life occupied by career and rearing a family, then phase three is that of teacher, contributor, helper, and friend.

I will not enjoy phase three if I try to convince myself that I am not really getting older, or if I think of it only as meant totally for my pleasure.

In phase three some people hit the wall and others hit their stride. Don't quit before God takes you out of His work force. Be able to say with Jesus, "I have brought you glory on earth by completing the work you gave me to do" (John 17:4).

The enjoyment of phase three comes in bringing together all that God has given and taught us, and then offering that to others.

Am I there yet? Yes, I am—or soon will be. I can take inventory, look at all that God has done for me, realize all my experience and training as well as opportunities to learn from my mistakes, and then offer all I am and all I am becoming to God. He will know where I am needed. And what better place to be than in God's will, putting to good use all that He has given me.

I am an investor for God of the talents He has placed in my hands. Whether He brings forth tenfold or fivefold, I will not deny what I have.

Robert Browning said it many years ago, but it is worth hearing again:

Grow old along with me! The best is yet to be,
The last of life, for which the first was made.

Like Browning, we will have that best in the last of life as we realize that God has been preparing us for this time of life and has a wonderful reason for our being here—right now.

For Reflection:

1. Do you think of yourself as old, tired, and without a future? Is that the way God thinks of you?

2. If you are retired or are about to be, have you offered yourself to God anew for the years ahead?

3. What has God been saying to you about the rest of your life?

4. What does Scripture say to you about the value of your life?

5. Who in your immediate area needs the gifts you have to offer? What about other parts of the country? What about the world?

Freedom to Be

2

"It is not how many years we live,
but what we do with them."
Evangeline Cory Booth

"We are always the same age inside."
Gertrude Stein

"I'm seventy-three years of age, but how do I retire in this kind of calling? What I thought would be an invitation to a few speaking dates here and there has turned into a deluge." Roger Fredrikson is a retired pastor. At least, that's what he thought he was. Instead, he is in demand everywhere for a ministry of renewal to the churches. "There is a tremendous hunger in the institutional churches for new life. And we're helping with that renewal, trying to overcome some of the obstacles, the institutional entrapment, the saying that 'We've always done it this way,' the spiritual apathy, lack of vision, and failure to take the Bible seriously." This man from Sioux

Falls, South Dakota is having an ongoing ministry after a successful career of Christian service. And, he is enjoying every minute of it.

Roger told me the story of Ruth, a survivor of Auschwitz who was a concert pianist in Berlin before she was captured by the Nazis. She lost her mother and father and twenty-two other family members in the death camps. Today she has one arm, so she plays the piano with that one hand. And, she gives piano lessons. Did she have a peaceful life, an easy life? Not at all. But she keeps on going. Like the rest of us, she still has much to give. Despite the pain of her past and the difficulties of the present, she has a freedom in her life. A freedom to be.

George Fooshee, a former bill collector, lives in Wichita, Kansas. He says, "In 1982 we sensed the Lord was saying, 'Change careers.' So, I put it on the calendar for December 31, 1987, five years later. We acted in faith because we didn't know what that meant. We were praying and knew the Lord would reveal something."

Today George Fooshee is director of the Midwest region and a board member of Crown Ministries, an organization which teaches biblical principles of money management, helps people set financial goals for themselves, and shows them how to establish a budget so that they can be free of debt and give more money to kingdom work. "A lot of our ministry is with young folks," George says. "It's exciting to watch lives change. I'm not retired, I'm rehired."

A People of Balance

When we are older, we want time to be quiet, to reflect, to enjoy new sights, to enjoy our hobbies, to take walks, and hold hands with the one we married so many years before. We have a right to enjoy nature; God provided it and then gave us our senses to appreciate it. And we want to have time for family and friends.

Because we are older, we want to be people of balance and understanding, free to be examples of action and peace, strength and security, in a time when so many people need those examples.

What is interesting to me about a man like Roger Fredrikson is that when he was young, he was a youth leader. As a mature adult he was one of the most effective pastors in his denomination. Now at age seventy-three, he is helping churches with renewal. He's telling them, "Get out of your rut. Change. Adjust. Adapt."

"Wait a minute," you say. "That's not what men in their seventies do; they are set in their ways, aren't they? Men in their seventies don't have new creative ways of thinking; they don't say, 'Get out of a rut.' Men in their seventies are *in* a rut, aren't they?"

Growing older is liberating. As we age we enter what psychologist Carl Jung called "the second half of life," and it's the better half because we don't have to prove anything anymore. We know who we are. We've discovered what works in our life and what doesn't. We have experienced the goodness of God in depths and dimensions that younger people haven't yet found. We can talk about those, live them, demonstrate them.

Look what we have going for us in our later years. We built our younger lives on what we learned from those before us. We practiced what they taught us. Then we added our own experiences. Now we've got the balance of both. We're free to be all that God designed us to be.

In the first half of life we really weren't so free. We were experimenting, trying, attempting to discover who we were. Now we are growing—and without all the entanglements and entrapments that grabbed us when we were younger. We understand biblical truth and know how it applies. As one person said, "I can be myself. I'm old enough to do that now."

But there's a false teaching that needs to be corrected. It's the teaching that old is old, retired is retired, when in fact old is a growing time based on all that has gone before, a liberating time to put into practice what we have learned in earlier years. Old age isn't meaningless; for many people it is the beginning of true meaning. And even when we're limited by physical disabilities, we can be teachers. We're old enough not to blame others for where we are, what we are, or who we are. We're old enough to take responsibility and show how to live out the life that God has given to us.

Ross Martin, a retired business executive, now works with prisoners at Stillwater Prison in Minnesota. He says, "I'm able to give the prisoners a positive father image which many didn't have from their own fathers. Many were rejected, beaten.

"Retirees have a world of experience, a testimony to offer. But so many allow it to rot when they reach sixty-five. I get so frustrated with some retirees. We have a life of experience that shouldn't go to waste."

Some people don't go happily into the future with God because they're too busy looking back to what used to be "in the good old days—when I was younger and I had my health." They're not free! They're looking forward with dread, saying, "I have nothing ahead of me but the grave. I'm going to have my worst illnesses in the years to come," and so they're not living successfully now. They not only miss out on the future, but they're not even free to enjoy the present.

But when we are free to be, we do live in the now. Illness isn't inevitable; we may have years more to serve in some way. Physical decline can be worse as an anticipation than as a reality. So we exercise, eat right, sleep enough hours, and get up in the morning with a heart that's pumping strong with enthusiasm for life. Our brains don't die. Someone has pointed out that Copernicus was seventy and Galileo sixty-eight when they did their most significant work. Somebody forgot to tell them that when you're older your mind doesn't work so well.

Three O'Clock in the Morning

Of course we get tired. We can't go as long between naps. We don't sleep as well at night. Fine. We recognize it and keep going.

I do very well sleeping the early part of the night, and then along about three o'clock in the morning, my mind begins to work on problems, real or imagined. I anticipate the new day, and recall what I should have done or could have done better the previous day.

At three o'clock in the morning I realize that I'm a contrast to what I preach and teach, because I do believe what Isaiah said, "You will keep in perfect peace him whose mind is steadfast, because he trusts in you" (Isaiah 26:3).

Steadfast mind? A trusting person? That's the one who has perfect peace, and perfect peace is God's peace. It isn't generated by us; it's given by God.

At three o'clock in the morning this verse doesn't always work itself out in my thinking. Yet I suspect that the formula for a whole night of rest is right there in that verse. "You will keep in perfect peace him whose mind is steadfast." Maybe I should repeat that each night just before I go to sleep.

Isaiah also said, "He will be the sure foundation for your times" (Isaiah 33:6). Is God my sure foundation, the stability of my times? Most of us are past being pushed and pulled by all that influenced us in our earlier years. We know where our stability is. We know that God is not shoved away by life's storms or our confusion or our circumstances or even our finances. God is not swept away by family problems or disabilities. He is the stability for our times, and that understanding gives us great freedom.

Ready to Volunteer

People say, "There is more volunteering going on today than ever." But others reply, "That's true, as long as the volunteer work fits a particular person's desire and schedule at that moment. But if someone volunteers an hour for a particular task, don't expect him to come back next week and volunteer another hour."

I ask myself where the faithful and steady volunteers are. Then in the New Testament, I read about a woman by the name of Dorcas, also known as Tabitha. Her volunteer work is described in Acts 9:36; she "was always doing good and helping the poor."

She wasn't a one-hour-a-week person. She wasn't an occasional if-it-suits-my-schedule person. She wasn't even the kind who did something only if it gave her a sense of satisfaction. She was "always doing good and helping the poor." What a reputation to have—abounding with deeds of kindness and charity. Always. No taking off for a few months to "do what I want to do for a while," leaving a gap in ministry. We see no complaints of, "When is somebody going to do something for me?" She was "always doing good and helping the poor."

When it comes to volunteering, what is your reputation? Are you preparing for retirement by also preparing lists of people whom you want to minister to, care for, and express love to? As you prepare to take your pension and as you examine your stock portfolio and study brochures about that long-desired cruise, are you also listing the volunteer services you will undertake?

Tom Young of Ridgewood, New Jersey is open and ready for God to lead. How will he serve? Like many people facing retirement, he doesn't fully know yet, but he's available.

"I was a consulting actuary, but I'm retired now and I don't know yet what I'm going to do. My wife, Liz, has been active in Bible Study Fellowship. She has been a teacher-leader for seven years. That's a gift she can continue.

"My gifts are more subtle. I'm not sure where they could be used, but I've been praying about this. We do what we're asked to do in the church and we'd respond positively to short-term ministry. We are in a position to support ourselves. I've been on the board of American Leprosy Mission for twelve years and have been active in that. Physically and emotionally it's not good for our health not to have anything challenging to do.

"We're concentrating on what to do. If an opportunity dictated a move, we'd be open. We're early on in this process, but it's an interesting phase in life."

Tom and Liz Young are retired and ready. God can work with people like that. The Apostle Paul was retired too, not by choice but of necessity. He was in jail, writing a particular thank-you letter that we call Philippians. Volunteers in Philippi had sent him a gift, probably some food and other necessities. Yet listen to this man as he writes his thank-you note, "I have received full payment and even more; I am amply supplied, now that I have received from Epaphroditus the gifts you sent. They are a fragrant offering, an acceptable sacrifice, pleasing to God" (Philippians 4:18).

My mouth drops open at that. Paul has so little, but he feels he has everything. To him, those volunteers had done so much.

Using himself as an example, Paul finishes his letter by saying, "And my God will meet all your needs according to his glorious riches in Christ Jesus" (v. 19). Just as He supplied all of mine, He will supply all of yours, he says. To Paul, these were not just physical gifts but spiritual gifts. Imagine their surprise when those volunteers learned from Paul's letter how much their help had meant to him.

Maybe we need to put this thank-you note of the Apostle Paul next to our list of volunteer services. It will put what we do in perspective.

Because We Have Hope

"But I don't have much hope for my retirement years," you say. "I feel I'm going to be on the shelf." Do you have Christ? Then you have everything you need. You do have hope. When people say they have no hope, tell them about Romans 5.

Romans 5:1 says, "Therefore, since we have been justified through faith, we have peace with God through our Lord Jesus Christ." But it doesn't stop there. It goes on to say, "Through whom we have gained access by faith into this grace in which we now stand. And we rejoice in the hope of the glory of God" (v. 2).

And then Paul talks about tribulation, "Not only so, but we also rejoice in our sufferings, because we know that suffering produces perseverance; perseverance, character; and character, hope. And hope does not disappoint us" (vv. 3-5).

Without faith in Christ, there is no hope. With faith in Christ, there is great hope, even when the journey to it goes through tribulations. So, if someone wants hope, take that person back to the introduction. The introduction is faith, and that gives peace with God through our Lord Jesus Christ. It's quite wonderful!

Trying to Be Faithful

If we will go around with our eyes open, we will see the opportunities for service that God wants us to see. Then when we see, it is up to us to do something about it.

Paul Baddour, a lawyer and a CPA, has "retired" to a whole new work. At first he served as Associate Director of World Evangelism, World Methodist Council. "In the summer of 1992 I met Dr. H. Eddie Fox, World Director of World Evangelism for the World Methodist Council, and he asked me to go to Europe with him. While in Eastern Europe we attended the Billy Graham Crusade in Moscow. When I saw half the audience going forward to accept Christ, I knew that I had to be involved in evangelism.

"With the World Methodist Council we have work in ninety-six countries. I am taking seminary professors to teach Christians in six to eight Eastern European countries. I'm involved in world evangelism.

"I wish other people working seventy to a hundred hours a week like I used to could be free of all that and direct their energy and stamina for the kingdom.

"I hope the Lord will use me as a witness and that I might help attract other people to the ministry. I'm just trying to be faithful." Today Paul Baddour continues in ministry, doing special projects for Asbury Theological Seminary.

Freedom to be is freedom to be ready, prepared, and able to say, "I'm going to trust You, God, to lead me to where You want me to serve." The psalmist said, "I wait for the Lord, my soul waits, and in his word I put my hope" (Psalm 130:5). Waiting and hoping constitute trust. It's not weakness to wait for God. It's not foolishness to hope.

We are waiting for all the parts to come together, parts that God understands. We're waiting for Him to work out not just the good, but the best. We're waiting for the fulfillment of His time. I think the psalmist had it right when he said, "My soul waits." Mine does too. We older folks have learned how to trust.

Questions We Need to Answer

One day in Sussex, England, I was visiting with Billy Strachan, principal of Capernwray Bible School and director of Radio Bible Class of Europe. As we walked together in the garden of Pilgrim Hall, where I was conducting a school of writing, we talked about the book that he should write. He did write it, a wonderful look at Paul the Apostle as seen through the Epistle to the Philippians. I won't quote the book—you can read it—but I will mention some of the questions that Billy Strachan asks you and me. Even if once we knew the answers to them, we need to look at them again, in this next stage of life.

Billy Strachan asks, "Do you claim your service as

your own? Do you wish you could be someone else instead of the unique you God made? Have you any gifts that you have never used? Are you caught up in your own little world? Are you running races that God did not intend for you?"[1]

These are questions we need to answer in every stage of life, and especially when we approach what some refer to as the glorious years but others refer to as the twilight years; years that launch some into a wonderful springtime of service and others into a time of decline; years that can be a phase three, building on all that went before, or years that are times of anger, frustration, criticism, loneliness, and hurt. We have gifts to use. How are we using them?

We Have Gifts—We Are Gifts

When the Apostle Paul talks about gifts he says, "Now to each one the manifestation of the Spirit is given for the common good" (1 Corinthians 12:7). No gift is given just for me. It is given for the body, for the church, for the good of the fellowship. The Apostle says in verse 11, "And he gives them to each one, just as he determines." The Holy Spirit decides what our gifts are to be. We can cultivate those gifts, develop and exercise them, but those gifts are exactly what the word means—gifts. They come from God.

God knows what He has given to me, and I am responsible for those gifts. God knows what He has given to you. You too are responsible for your gifts for the sake of the body, so that together we can bring all the gifts to bear within the fellowship.

Use your gift and rejoice in it. Thank God for your gift. He gave it to you, and He knew what He was doing.

We don't have a shallow religion. We live with a dynamic, powerful faith that is built on knowing who God is and what He can do in our lives. We've lived long enough to see it; we've experienced it.

Freedom to be me as a person in Christ means I have the freedom to show how a person ages in Christ. I have freedom to show how to shift directions, freedom to show how to trust God, freedom to give myself to others, freedom to be a witness without fear, freedom to verify that it's true as the Scripture says, "I was young and now I am old, yet I have never seen the righteous forsaken or their children begging bread" (Psalm 37:25).

We're free to no longer have to ask, "What if" this or "What if" that, as we did when we were younger. "What if I'd had a different education? What if I'd been born to a different family? What if I'd lived at another time? What if I'd had more opportunities? What if I didn't look the way I do?" Now we are free to be who we are and thank God for it. We're free because we know that God is much larger and greater than we ever thought He was.

Freedom to be means I have jettisoned a lot of the baggage, the cargo that made sailing in this life so difficult in the earlier years. I can give that up and be what God intended for me to be all along—free!

Free to Let Go of the Baggage

Given the choice, what some of us would really like is to have everything we want, without any storms in life, and enjoy the help of God. That's not always the way things go. It certainly wasn't for the Apostle Paul when he was shipwrecked, and I think what happened on that ship tells us something about our lives as well.

We read of that voyage in Acts 27:18, "We took such a violent battering from the storm." (Sometimes violent storms come up in our lives too. You've experienced it and so have I.) "We took such a violent battering from the storm that the next day they began to throw the cargo overboard." It may be that we have to get rid of a lot of things too. We don't like to hear that. Certainly the ship's captain didn't want to hear of it. That cargo going overboard was his profit for his company, but it had to be done. Then they threw over the ship's tackle. They didn't even have anything left to navigate with, but they survived.

That may be a description of life for you. You may be down to the tackle and that has to go also. And you may be thinking, "How much more will be taken from me?" God delivered them, minus cargo, minus tackle. But God delivered them.

Nobody wants to be storm-tossed. Nobody appreciates the pains of life. All of us would like to sail through without having to jettison any of our cargo, but we have no guarantees about that. The only guarantee we have is that God will deliver. Therefore, our job is to do what Paul told the others to do: keep up your courage; believe God. Then let that other "stuff" go.

In our later years we are free to come back to the basics, to the true values. That's what it means to be free in Christ.

Thousands of years ago the Prophet Habakkuk recognized what many of us are still learning.

> Though the fig tree does not bud
> and there are no grapes on the vines,
> though the olive crop fails
> and the fields produce no food,

though there are no sheep in the pen
and no cattle in the stalls,
yet I will rejoice in the Lord,
I will be joyful in God my Savior
                              (Habakkuk 3:17-18).

You can paraphrase that, "Though there is an old car
in the garage, though the income is smaller than I had
hoped, though the taxes are higher and the interest rates
lower, though my health is failing, yet I will rejoice in
the Lord and the God of my salvation."

When we can say that and mean it, then we are ready
to live. Then we are really free.

For Reflection:

1. Are you free right now to obey God's call? What will
it take for you to become free?

2. How do you view your circumstances, your economic, physical, and family responsibilities? Are they keeping you from ministry or giving you new avenues for
service?

3. In this chapter, whose story is for you the best example of being free? Could you be like that person?

4. What part of your life ministry causes you to be most thankful? Why is that?

5. Do others see your freedom to be? Do they recognize that your freedom begins in Christ? How will you tell them so that they'll be able to have the same freedom?

I'm Still Climbing

3

"Few people know how to be old."
François, Duc de la Rochefoucould

"Today I entered on my eighty-second year and found myself just as strong to labor and as fit for any exercise of body or mind as I was forty years ago."
John Wesley

Three weeks before his eighty-fifth birthday, George Beverly Shea, America's beloved Gospel singer, was in Tokyo, Japan at Mission '94 with Billy Graham.

As he stood to sing before that 40,000-plus audience in the Tokyo Dome, his rich bass-baritone voice communicated not only in English but in Japanese. He had learned the Japanese words to his songs. My interpreter leaned over and said to me, "His pronunciation is very good." Age is not a hindrance to learning new things.

When Maynard Johnson, now living in Florida, returned from teaching in Cameroon with his wife, Thelma,

I asked him about their retirement ministry. He said, "We were stretched there in so many ways—physically, because we walked instead of going by vehicle. We were stretched intellectually; when I taught I had the only textbook and made mimeographed sheets, but the students did learn.

"I was stretched emotionally, to be far from family and from conveniences, and also from seeing the people's needs. And I was stretched spiritually, to realize that God could use us in a land where the cultures and traditions were unfamiliar to us. I saw God work in people's lives in more ways than I ever thought possible. I was blessed by people singing the song, 'I'm Going Where You Want Me to Go, Lord,' and it spoke to me. Our lives have been changed. We feel we will never be the same again."

When Maynard and Thelma left Cameroon, they were asked, "Will you be back?" He reminded the people of his age. They replied, "Well, Moses started at age eighty."

Will they go back? They might. Maynard asked his doctor, "What about our health?" The doctor replied, "Well, you have to die somewhere. Why not in Africa?" Their doctor is right. Why not?

We all have new adventures to take, new worlds to conquer, new mountains to climb. We once climbed other mountains—education and business or professional success. We've built cars or houses. We've prepared roads or taken a private company public or taught school. We've performed delicate surgery or produced annual reports. We've climbed lots of mountains. But now we're retired, or about to be. Now it's time to start climbing other mountains, the ones that may bring more satisfaction, more lasting value than anything we've done before.

In an article in *Psychology Today*, Gilbert Brin, Ph.D., talked about his dad who had died a few days before. He said, "This man was as happy and fulfilled at 101 as he was at 60. He had an unyielding drive for growth and mastery, a rational mind, and a capacity for change."

Who? Me?

Why do we turn positives like old age into negatives? We hear people say, "Oh, I am so weak. I'm old, you know." Of course, you are. The question is, "How's your faith?" Who, me? Yes, you. Are you in the faith? If you are in the faith, the power of God is directed toward you, is working in you. Your strength or His? That's the question.

So the next time somebody comes to you and says, "I'm not very strong," you can reply, "Good. Now you can rely on the power of God." Esther Matteson of Royal Oak, Michigan is relying on the power of God. She hasn't let the years steal her capacity to learn and serve. "Soon, I will complete fifty years with Wycliffe Bible Translators. I haven't retired. I doubt that Christians serving the Lord ever really retire."

She worked in Spanish much of her life, and then in the Piro language. After retirement, she said, "I learned Russian, because we were trying to do work in Russia. It's not too much to learn a language when you're older. Since then I have learned two more related languages. You can learn to speak a language when you're older if you've kept on using your mind. I have friends who started languages in their late sixties and learned to speak fluently. I have the motivation, and as long as I'm still productive, I want to keep with it."

Cliff Jantzen is still climbing too. He's helping launch a

new church on a different model than the traditional church. He says, "I'm moderator of the provincial conference of Mennonite Brethren Churches. I'm also on the Executive Board of the Canadian Conference. Because of that ministry, my wife and I find ourselves involved in launching a new church here in Saskatchewan. We see the benefit of setting the old aside and we are committed to the open church, the cell group church."

About his previous work Cliff says, "I viewed my career in public education as a teacher, principal, and school division director as a ministry. When I retired in 1985, I became the president of Bethany Bible College, where I served without remuneration for six years."

How did he find the new work that God wanted for him when he retired? "During the last few years of my career, I was seeking the Lord's direction. For a month, I committed a specific time each day to seeking the mind of God. Bethany was a tremendously stretching experience, and that reshaped my thinking in terms of commitment to God. Anything we can do for the Lord will never repay His love."

Cliff Jantzen is still climbing. "I tend to be on the front end of change. I've always been quick to pick up on something new."

Climbing Even When You Think You Can't

Retirement offers wonderful challenges, but that doesn't mean it's a life without problems. You don't have to visit with too many people before somebody explodes, "If God is really God, I wouldn't have to go through all this suffering." Or, "Where is God when there are all these troubles in the world?" But when we hear that, we turn to those words in Isaiah 43:2, "When you pass through the waters, I will be with you; and when you pass through the rivers, they will not sweep over you."

Because we're in this world, we will go through the waters. Even in retirement, if we are investing our lives in kingdom work, we will face some raging rivers. Will we face them on our own? Or will we face them in the power of God with the assurance, "I will be with you"? The rest of that verse is, "When you walk through the fire, you will not be burned; the flames will not set you ablaze." You will walk through fire. I don't know what it will be—financial loss, cancer—but the flame won't burn you. You'll come out on the other side. That's God's assurance.

Until we leave this earth and meet our Christ in heaven, we will walk through fire and the waters. The question is, "Will we also be able to say with full confidence and assurance, 'He is with me'?" I don't know what's coming next in my life, but I do know that when troubles come, God says, "I will be with you."

David Carmichael of White Rock, British Columbia isn't looking for an easy life. As he prepares for retirement, he can hardly wait to start something new.

"As a believer, I must have purpose in my life. I'm not looking for ease. In North America we are so blessed that it is incumbent to offer ourselves to do something for the kingdom, to make a contribution. We can still play a little golf, but we should let God use all of our gifts and abilities and experiences.

"I don't want to dry up. I could go fifteen or twenty years if the Lord keeps me healthy. What distresses me is people in their seventies and eighties who have given up and become couch potatoes, concerned only about themselves.

"What really challenges me and gives me great inspiration is people in their nineties who are still making a contribution in other people's lives and in the kingdom."

Hitting the Wall

Most of us have been reared to believe that work has value only when it generates wealth. That's because we don't understand working for God. We tend to believe that even physical exercise or prayer has value only because it enables us to see immediate results. We have not always understood that God wants us near Him, attached as the vine to the branch, so that He can do a work through us. That's why He brought us to this place in our walk of faith.

We have to make a mental switch. We're not working for money anymore; we're giving ourselves away now. That's tough to grasp for someone burned out from years of earning a living. It's tough to say to people struggling to make ends meet by continuing to work part time after retirement. It's hard for that one who was always battling to climb the corporate ladder, and now he doesn't want to climb anymore. It's tough to say "serve" to one who wants only to take his leisure, because he's tired of the struggle.

The answer we need is not based on physical or emotional circumstances. The answer is spiritual. Quite simply, we're not finished yet. We're in a marathon and we may have "hit the wall," but that's all it is.

Have you hit the wall yet? You know what the wall is . . . runners hit it in a marathon. They are going along well, and suddenly they just run out of steam; they have no more in them. They start to stagger. And then it seems they get a second wind. That happens to people spiritually too.

Jesus talked to Peter about that. He said, "I have prayed for you, Simon, that your faith may not fail." In other words, "that you will be able to keep on going." He actually allows for faith to hit the wall and a second breath to come; He says, "And when you have turned back, strengthen your brothers" (Luke 22:32). "Peter, once you get back your wind, once you have turned the corner, once you have overcome your weaknesses, once you have been strengthened again, I have a job for you—to strengthen other people."

We are not in this race only for ourselves. We are to strengthen our brothers and sisters running alongside us. You may be getting a second wind in order to reach out and pull somebody else along, just as they may have reached out and pulled you along. God gives us new bursts of faith. We hit the wall and think we can't go on. But we *can* go on, and because He is the strength-giver, we can then offer strength to somebody else.

Jesus told Peter how to do it. He tells us how to do it. Your race isn't finished yet. You may be just getting your second wind. When you do, there is somebody who needs your help.

Claire Miller of Ontario, Canada understands that. He's still climbing. "I retired keeping in mind that I wanted to be in construction helping missionaries. The first summer I went to Medellín, Colombia to help with construction at a Bible school.

"Then I helped at JAARS, Jungle Aviation and Radio Service, in Waxhaw, North Carolina where I supervised the construction of an office and classrooms.

"Since retirement I've gone into the high Arctic three times, and that was a wonderful experience. There I taught an apprenticeship training program for Inuits in the Northwest Territories. We were also renovating government housing, and also helped renovate a training center for the Anglican church, where they prepare Inuit men to be ministers in the Anglican Church in the Arctic.

"With our Fellowship Evangelical Baptist Church construction group, I supervise the carpenters on these construction jobs. We can usually complete a church in a week. It's exciting!

"I'm sixty-seven, and I realize I have to do more supervision and less of the physical, though it doesn't bother me to climb around with the rest of the men. In fact, I find that if I don't get in and work with them, I can't give supervision. Later, when I'm older, they won't expect an old man to work with them. Then they might accept only supervision from me.

"We've built six churches recently: two in Nova Scotia, two in Ontario, one in British Columbia, and one in Alberta. This summer we hope to build a small church on an Indian reserve up near Owen Sound, a house for a missionary friend near Ottawa, and a church at Wallaceburg, Ontario.

"I believe that it is never good for one to quit work. I see a real need, and the Lord has blessed me so I can do these things."

A missionary/theologian who serves in Brazil says that in theological education he needs the help of retirees too. "To know God and make him known—is there anything more exciting? There are so many opportunities. People need to find out where they can serve by talking with their own denominational leaders and mission boards.

"That North Americans are interested in them and would pay their own way to go means so much to Brazilians! Presence is such an encouragement. Retirees could teach English to lay people or seminary students, since they all want to learn English. They could teach Bible studies, give lectures, or teach in seminary classes. But there is also music and construction. Most of all, the presence of North Americans is so welcome."

I'd Serve Too, If God Were Blessing Me

"But you don't know what I'm facing. You don't know my struggles. I can't keep climbing." There are people who deep down are thinking, "God hasn't really blessed me." They may not say it publicly, but they say it in their own souls. "If God were really blessing me, I wouldn't have these family problems, I wouldn't have these financial needs, I wouldn't be struggling socially. I wouldn't be feeling physical pain . . . not if God were really blessing me."

Then someone comes right back and says, "But He has blessed you with all spiritual blessings."

"But I can't measure that. What spiritual blessings? How can I know?"

We really can measure spiritual blessings, but not in the same way we measure everything else. The Apostle Paul told the Ephesian church, "Praise be to the God and Father of our Lord Jesus Christ, who has blessed us in the heavenly realms with every spiritual blessing in Christ" (Ephesians 1:3).

They're there, those blessings. They're ours, and they are gaining interest. We'll know it the moment we turn from looking at the so-called negatives and start looking at God. "Praise be to the God and Father of our Lord Jesus Christ," Paul said. Praise opens our eyes to blessing. The question is not, "Do we have the spiritual blessings?" We have them. The question is, "Will we recognize them and praise God for them?" If we don't, we'll always be taking inventory of other things, and feel that we have come up short.

A fallacy that catches me every now and again goes like this. If I had the power of King David, think what I could do. If I had the wealth of King David, think of where I would be. Or, if I had David's strength, and so on. . . .

But I know that is wrong thinking when I read Psalm 25, which was written by David. "The troubles of my heart have multiplied" (v. 17). *Trouble* means "distress." Now think of that! Here is a man who had it all and yet, he says, "The troubles of my heart have multiplied." It is as if troubles had moved in, making more and more room for themselves and pushing out the sides of his heart so that his heart was hurting. This Scripture literally is saying, "My heart is trouble."

I'm glad he wrote that. I am glad that he didn't go through life saying, "Oh, I'm fine, thank you." David knew the pain of a troubled heart. Life wasn't like that for him all of the time, of course. It isn't like that for us all of the time either, but when our heart hurts, we feel as if the distress is just pushing the sides out.

Like David, we don't stop at the distress, for we can pray with him, "Free me from my anguish. Look upon my affliction and my distress and take away all my sins" (Psalm 25:17-18). That is the answer for a troubled heart.

We Don't Retire from Problems

Perhaps you thought that with retirement you would eliminate all of the problems that you once associated with your working career, but still they continue. You're under stress even as you communicate with your children who are under stress, or your neighbors and friends.

Your plans are upset. Life is suddenly turned over. From your years of experience, you have some perspective that helps you understand what is happening, but still you must face it.

One of the great pleasures I have is teaching at the Billy Graham Schools of Evangelism. I love to talk with pastors, but I also find that there is a great deal of over-work and pain among the clergy. I think it's because there is never a sense of closure. That is, there is always more work to be done, more people with needs, more individuals to be counseled, further preparation for teaching. One can't go home at night and say, "Well, I've completed the day's work," because often at the end of the day there's more work waiting than was completed.

It can be the same for retirees. "I thought I'd have less to worry about. Where's the ease I thought was waiting for me when I retired? I don't have fewer problems than when I was going to work every day. I have more."

Zechariah 4:6 is a verse of peace in times like this, " 'Not by might nor by power, but by my Spirit,' says the Lord Almighty."

No matter what we do, working in a profession or living in a retirement community, we recognize that we can't function in our own might or power. It's the Holy Spirit who gives us the strength to keep going and the discernment about what to do and what not to do in difficult situations.

Charles Grierson keeps going, even though he could give in to the health problems that made him retire. He hasn't done that because he sees too many men around who need God.

"I was a hospital administrator when I retired. What brought me to retirement six years ago was a heart attack followed by a mild stroke. The Lord got my attention. But, as soon as I retired, I had the need to draw men into the church and then give them something that ministers to them. So I took on the job of coordinator of men's work for the British Columbia area of the Baptist Union of Western Canada. I brought to this volunteer position my many years in church as a layman and thirty years in health care administration.

"The work with men came without a job description, so I started from scratch. I will continue doing this as long as my health permits.

"I have noticed in the shopping malls how many retired men are just sitting on the benches. So right now we are investigating something new, a witness program for men in the shopping centers."

Are you working in the power of God's Spirit or in your own power? Is it by God's might or by your might? You'll always feel you have too much to do if you're faithful. It's the Spirit of God who can tell you what to do now, what to postpone, and what not to do. And, when the Spirit of God tells you what to do, it's by His power that you will be able to do it. We come to learn that there is not always closure, that the most we can say sometimes is, "I've done all that I can for now," and leave the next steps to God.

A Mental Picture for Me

We often quote Psalm 23, but I am not sure that we always understand it. For example, if you have a good mind for picture language, look at Psalm 23:6, "Surely goodness and love (mercy) will follow me all the days of my life, and I will dwell in the house of the Lord forever."

Now we don't have much trouble understanding the last part, "I will dwell in the house of the Lord forever." That is eternal! Jesus told us about a house with many mansions and that He is preparing a place there for us.

It is the first part that I am not sure we always see, "Surely goodness and love will follow me all the days of my life." God is goodness and love. He is right there with bundles in His arms—bundles of goodness and bundles of love—with my name on them.

We think that we have to cry out to God, "Where is Your mercy? Where is Your goodness? Why can't I find it?" when all of the time God is right there—every step of the way—with His goodness and love. It is goodness that He wants to give me. It is mercy that He wants to show me.

He wants it for you too. During the next day or two, try to picture God right there beside you, or just one step ahead of you, with His gifts of goodness and love. You will feel the blessing and you will sense the strength. It will change the way you act and the way you think. And you will find yourself saying, "I feel so secure."

Start looking at those difficulties in your climbing as reasons for prayer, opportunities to seek the bundles of goodness and grace and mercy, the help of God.

For a period of several weeks, I had to drive in England and Scotland. When I drive there, I pray a lot, especially at the roundabouts when I'm trying to watch traffic and find the correct road sign at the same time. It's a good experience.

The Apostle Paul wasn't driving a car in Britain or anywhere else, but he told us to pray without ceasing. "Pray continually" (1 Thessalonians 5:17). When things are easy or comfortable or ordinary and we're on mental automatic, we don't talk as much with God. We just assume we can handle whatever will happen. But not when things change. There's something to be said for driving on the other side of the road. I need to see all of life as driving on the other side of the road, so that I'll be alert to my need. Then maybe I'll pray continually.

Jim Lucas found himself "on the other side of the road" when he came home from many years in Africa and faced culture shock. To start a new ministry in North America, he had to learn new witnessing techniques.

"My wife and I were career missionaries in Africa for thirty years with the Sudan Interior Mission, first in Nigeria and then in Niger Republic. In 1982 we returned to the States to retire. But I wanted to continue in ministry since my health was fairly good.

"Today I'm working in the Highlands County Jail in Sebring, Florida as a volunteer chaplain. For a time I was having classes in the cell block. I've had as many as eleven men, some sitting on their beds, some on the toilet and some on the floor. But mostly I'm doing one-on-one. We have Sunday church services too. One Mexican man who received Christ early in my work was released, went to Bible school, and has come back to minister to the Hispanic prisoners.

"In one cell there was a breakout. Guards caught three of the escapees right away, but the fourth was loose for a week.

"The next Sunday, coming out of a church service, I was invited to solitary. I talked to one of the fellows who had broken out, and another in the next cell said, 'Come over here so I can hear too.' I witnessed to him. We began to have meetings there and later others came in and some were converted. It was really rewarding.

"I'm praying the Lord will let me do this as long as I can. I don't want to stop; I'm enjoying it too much."

Jim Lucas is still climbing.

Spiritual Lessons for Climbers

The psalmist asked God, "Will You not revive us again, that your people may rejoice in you?" (Psalm 85:6) God does revive us again and again and again. A wonderful thing about God is that we keep finding new blessings from Him, especially when we are climbing new mountains.

As I meet with directors of mission-sending agencies or talk to retirees who are committed, growing, and serving, I find myself exclaiming, "The blessings are everywhere for us to enjoy. With God, our aging just opens new doors."

When I turned fifty-seven, I counted the months until age sixty, sixty-three and sixty-five, not because I wanted to leave my work but because I felt like a marathon runner. It was time to give a kick, to shift into higher gear. Some people start to coast. I have no intention of coasting. I got my first paying job on my tenth birthday. At age sixty I will have worked fifty years. Whenever "retirement" comes, I will not stop.

I plan a phase-three, post-retirement ministry. To be ready for it, I'm putting on that extra speed now. It is time to pick up the pace, not slow it down.

"Easy for you," someone may say. "I'm way too old." And I reply, "Too old for what?" and remind them of another person who was "too old" for something new— Abraham's wife Sarah. Don't talk about "too old."

Sarah laughed. After all, she was ancient and so was Abraham. How could there be a child for them? God asked, "Why did you laugh?" She replied, "Oh, I didn't laugh."

God knows when we are laughing at what He says, when we are mocking His assurances and promises. God knows when we read His Word and say, "Impossible!" God knows when we say we are too old to pray about new opportunities, because we have already decided that He is incapable of answering.

Sarah did laugh. And God's reply to her is the same one He makes to us when we say, "Impossible! It's beyond my comprehension; therefore, God, it must be beyond Your ability."

God said, "Is anything too hard for the Lord?" (Genesis 18:14) Now think about that. Anything? This is the God of the ages, the Lord of the universe, the God of all creation—your Creator too. He made Sarah and Abraham. Could He recreate and make it possible for them to have a child? Of course He could. And He did.

Open to Take a Chance

Is there anything in your life too difficult for God? Can He renew what He established in the first place? Can He recreate what He created once before? Is there anything about you or your circumstances or your surroundings that is too difficult for God? What is it that you have refused to talk to God about because you are thinking, "That's impossible"? Well, according to what God says, it isn't impossible. What are you waiting for? Why don't you talk to Him about that right now?

A management labor relations attorney by the name of Donald C. Duck lives in Indianapolis, Indiana. When I chatted with him he was seventy-eight years old. He said, "I became a Christian in February 1962. I had spent the first forty-six years of my life thinking I didn't need any help, thank you." Shortly after his conversion he became involved in Faith at Work in Indianapolis and also helped to start similar programs in Kentucky, Illinois, Ohio, and Michigan. At the same time he began working with Camps Farthest Out and continued doing that for years.

In 1984, Donald had a call to work with a rescue mission, serving on their board. He said, "I believe that I was being nudged into rescue mission work," and he's still on the board of the Lighthouse Mission in Indianapolis.

That mission has expanded into ministry to the homeless, and he's helping with that expansion. He's also involved in ministry in his church.

It's Donald's attitude that impresses me. He hasn't stopped climbing. He said, "I'm seventy-eight now and I have a few physical difficulties. I've had two spine operations and two eye operations in the last six months, but I'm ready for whatever's ahead. I'm sure I'm not an easy person for the Lord to penetrate in mind and heart, but I hope I'll be open to take a chance on whatever it is God wants me to do. I know I won't be doing it in my own strength."

He's right. God says to him and to us, "Whatever your hand finds to do, do it with all your might, for in the grave, where you are going, there is neither working nor planning nor knowledge nor wisdom" (Ecclesiastes 9:10).

We aren't in the grave yet. So we can keep on climbing. And, with God's help, the last part of the climb can be the best part of the climb.

"They will still bear fruit in old age, they will stay fresh and green" (Psalm 92:14).

For Reflection:

1. Have you told God, "That's impossible"? Do you want to change your mind about that?

2. What new mountain should you be climbing right now? What are you waiting for?

3. Whom do you know who can introduce you to a new ministry? Isn't it time you called that person?

4. Have you taken inventory of your gifts? If you ask your pastor, denominational executives, or mission board leaders how you can be used, what do you think they'll say?

5. This is the day to start climbing. What's the first new thing you will do today to get started?

Pupil, Teacher— Now I'm Both

4

*"To know how to grow old is the master work of wisdom
and one of the most difficult chapters in the
great art of living."*
Henri Frédéric Amiel

*"Anyone who stops learning is old,
whether at twenty or eighty."*
Author unknown

It was a visit I had been looking forward to, and I wasn't
disappointed. Warner R. Cole, for many years distin-
guished minister of Covenant Baptist Church, Detroit,
Michigan, was living in a retirement community in Cali-
fornia. Mrs. Cole had passed away and he was alone.

He greeted me eagerly at the door, ushered me in for
a visit, and surprised me. I half expected that our conversation would be reminiscences of years past, of the
days of Covenant Baptist Church, of the early Billy Graham Crusade he chaired, but not so. He was interested

in contemporary issues, particularly their theological implications. And I noticed that the books he was reading, scattered on his book table, were not dusty tomes from former days of ministry but were new releases—books just then making their mark, subjects that university and seminary students were beginning to wrestle with.

It was my last visit with Dr. Cole, who had been my pastor during my student years. He died shortly after that visit. But I will always have in my mind the remembrance of him as a reader of the contemporary, a student of the issues of the day, a man not just keeping up but being in the vanguard of thought.

To me Warner Cole disproved the myth that we can't learn as we grow older. Many who say that they can't learn probably were not particularly eager to learn when they were younger either. Every teacher knows that some students want to take the easy way. Every employer has been frustrated by an employee who says he wants to learn but really wants someone else to do the difficult tasks for him. So, maybe what we are when we are older is not so much a result of aging as it is an extension of what we were when we were younger.

Roy Robertson hasn't lived very many years in his home state of Texas, not since he left to become a fighter pilot in World War II. For most of his life he has lived and worked in Asia, first with the Navigators, now organizing evangelistic teams throughout Asia. They go out with the Gospel, some to their own people, some cross-culturally. Roy travels from country to country encouraging these evangelists.

He says, "You can learn new things. I'm seventy-two and I'm having a new thrust I didn't have thirty years ago. Today I learn Scripture even better than I did then. You can train your mind and it will improve. My wife and I learned Tagalog after age sixty. We learned Cantonese after age sixty-five." He already knows five languages and wants to learn one of the languages of India.

And that's not all. He says, "When I was sixty-nine, I decided to start studying tennis with a professional because I wanted to improve my game. Even though I've played tennis all my life, this professional reconstructed my game. He said, 'You work harder than the teenagers!' That's true, because I know what I want; I'm motivated.' "

Stretching or Vegetating?

Loving God is a mental exercise. We don't often think of it that way, but it is. We are to love the Lord with all our mind, and that means regardless of our level of education or experience, we can learn more. It's an act of dedication to focus our minds on loving and serving God.

Is your mind being stretched so that you have a greater and greater capacity to love and serve God? Or, are you vegetating so that you have less and less mental capacity to offer Him?

Jesus said, " 'Love the Lord your God with all your heart and with all your soul and with all your mind' " (Matthew 22:37). All of it! I know people who think that mind and faith are incompatible. I wonder what they love God with.

In retirement there is time and opportunity to be witnesses to Christ as perhaps never before. You don't know enough Bible? You wish you understood the New Testament better? Fine. Take a correspondence course from a Bible school or, better yet, attend one in your area or enroll at a nearby theological seminary. Ask your pastor for books that will help you. You don't stop growing just because you're no longer on a payroll. In fact, retirement gives opportunity to grow in directions you didn't before, and to do things you never had a chance to do.

Just as job training is important before we go to work, and on-the-job training is crucial while we are employed, so we need training for offering the Gospel. We are not only presenters of the Good News but teachers of the next generation of Good News presenters. Paul told Timothy, "And the things you have heard me say in the presence of many witnesses entrust to reliable men who will also be qualified to teach others" (2 Timothy 2:2).

Our responsibility is to teach those around us the truths of God in such a way that they not only can believe and apply them to their own lives but can pass those truths on to other people. If we miss this opportunity or decide not to take it, a whole generation may pass through without hearing the truths of the Gospel message. Or, if they know the truth, they will not know how to present it in the marketplace of their day.

"The things you have heard me say in the presence of many witnesses entrust to reliable men who will also be qualified to teach others," Paul said. Not strange esoteric teachings, but the Gospel. That is what we are to pass on so that those who learn from us will in turn be able to teach others also.

I am grateful that Paul taught Timothy, and Timothy taught others, and those others taught the many who went before me. Now I have an obligation to teach those coming along behind me.

We Aren't Babies

I know some people who haven't grown much in the last forty, fifty, or sixty years. Some haven't done any serious reading since they left high school or college. We can atrophy as persons if we don't exercise our skills, abilities, gifts, and the brains God gave us. We are pupils, but we are also teachers. We are not babies.

The other day I met a one-week-old baby and I wanted to hold him, care for him, and feed him. We feel that way about babies in Christ too, new believers. But there are people who have been Christians for thirty or fifty years who think they are still cute babies. They want to be held and fed. They are just too immature to make it on their own. They take in, but they don't give out. The Book of Hebrews describes them:

> Though by this time you ought to be teachers, you need someone to teach you the elementary truths of God's word all over again. You need milk, not solid food! Anyone who lives on milk, being still an infant, is not acquainted with the teaching about righteousness. But solid food is for the mature, who by constant use have trained themselves to distinguish good from evil (5:12-14).

By the time a Christian reaches several years in the faith, he ought to be well past the spiritual milk stage; yet, some continue to want the simple things. They don't want to grow. They don't want to deepen in the Word. As a result, they don't know much about God or understand biblically what's going on around them. They are just babies—and not cute either. In fact, a grown-up baby is not cute at all.

It Isn't Just for Us

Learning, using our minds, isn't just for us. Why did God put us on this earth? Why did He give us the ability to learn, if not to be mentors, teachers, and people who use our gifts and skills to help others?

Bert Friesen of White Rock, British Columbia is doing that. He was a hospital administrator before he retired. Then he and his wife, Marie, went to Africa.

"We spent a three-and-one-half-year term in Swaziland at the Nazarene Medical Mission in Manzini where the church has a 300-bed hospital along with fifteen rural clinics and a nurses' training school. Later we spent another fifteen-month term in Swaziland at the same medical mission. We felt needed and were happy to be able to pass on some of our experience and skills to the local people in their struggle to become self-sufficient.

"Also, we felt useful in being able to relieve the career missionaries so that they could get away for a much-needed furlough. A good example of this was a month we spent in South Africa being house-parents in a home for missionary children from all over southern Africa. This enabled the permanent house-parents to go home to the United States to attend their son's wedding.

"While working at the hospital, I coached the local Swazi administrator in his job and covered for him while he was away in England for two years for further training. I also taught accounting and supervisory skills to the hospital department heads. Marie helped the local church people open a Gospel bookstore and run it on an economical basis.

"We felt that everything we had ever learned and experienced in our working careers was useful in this developing country. God was allowing us to pass on to others some of what we knew.

"We are contented and have a healthy feeling of self-worth in the work God is leading us to do. We are having a happy and fulfilled retirement."

People Helping Other People

Writing in the ACMC (Advancing Churches in Mission Commitment) *Networker*, Bill Waldrop described something that is happening in our churches.

> The world mission enterprise from the American church is now being funded almost entirely by people who are approaching retirement, already retired, or nearing the end of life. Responsibility for dealing with this situation falls largely to the older generation. . . . There is a great lack of mentoring in the churches. Older men and women should be investing their lives in younger men and women, sharing the wealth of their Christian maturity and experience.[1]

That's our work, our obligation, and our opportunity. We are mentors. And, because you and I are potentially always teaching, we're constantly studying too. Pupil/teacher — they go hand in hand. Aging carries us forward. We are not going downhill, but onward. We are growing, stretching, maturing, and all of that makes us gifts to other people. We have much to offer.

When they reach a certain age, some people continue to take in but no longer see the necessity to give what they know to other people. Others, although they want to give what they know, are not taking in or learning. This means they're repeating lessons learned twenty or thirty years ago, and are not contemporary. Soon, no one is hearing them anymore. People who are true pupil/teachers are both learning and giving; they are excited by what they're gaining and also by what they're giving. They like the results they see in others.

We all should have someone into whom we are pour-

ing our life. We should have people coming along behind in various stages of Christian growth who are being helped by us. Perhaps it is someone we brought to
faith. Perhaps it is someone needing help. We invest in
other people, for this is what it means to be a true minister of the Gospel.

The Apostle Paul told us all about it. Paul was a teacher who said, "How can we thank God enough for you in
return for all the joy we have in the presence of our God
because of you?" (1 Thessalonians 3:9)

How can I thank God for the rejoicing that I have
because of you, your faith, your growth, and your activity for the Gospel? And then he said, "Night and day we
pray most earnestly that we may see you again and supply what is lacking in your faith" (v. 10). He knew what
some of us can still learn—the joy of encouraging, helping, teaching others, and supplying to them what is still
lacking.

Who are you trying to help to grow in the Lord, to
help them make up what might be lacking in their faith?
Let's turn that around. Who is helping you? For no one
is so mature in the faith that he doesn't need more help
himself.

Are you investing in the lives of other believers? Are
you allowing others to invest in you? Part of the joy we
have in Christ is that we get to pray for each other and
help bring one another along to completion in Christ
Jesus. No one in Christ is beyond learning. And no one
is without a ministry to someone else. All of us have
something to invest in another. What investment are
you making in others right now? And if you are not,
when are you going to start?

We are to be trained and we are to be trainers, or else
we will be only inwardly focused. We grow the most as

we grow for and with others. In so doing, we are blessed ourselves even as we are a blessing to others. We love and are loved; we give, we take, then we give some more.

Giving more is what Walter Lint is doing. For years he gave himself as a science teacher. He's still giving. He explains, "I tutor young people in the Family Life Center sponsored by the Union Gospel Mission in Winnipeg. The center has a school to help native young people upgrade their education. Many have come off the reservations and have not completed their high school education.

"I spend a day a week tutoring there. I find it very profitable to be in contact with the young people. The volunteer teachers attempt to bring them up to high school level and prepare them for further education. They can earn a G.E.D., a grade twelve standing.

"As a former teacher, I find it very satisfying and rewarding to help these young people with their education. One young man I'm helping is from Guyana in South America. He wants to be an auto mechanic. A young lady I helped last year has gone on to community college. She needed help with grade eleven algebra.

"Many whom I tutor are in their twenties; some are even older, with families. There is no such thing as a discipline problem because they all mean business.

"I feel that part of my duty as a believer is to make use of my talents to help other people.

"I'm seventy-eight. I think I can go on for a while yet. I find tutoring helps me in my thinking and my alertness. It's a challenge. I have to move along pretty fast to come up with answers when they are required. I feel the Lord has given me a talent to teach. I love explaining things to people."

Called to Encourage

When I finished reading *Inside Out: The Rise and Fall of Wall Street Traders*, it struck me that the men told about in this book, many of whom ended up in jail for insider trading, were working the Wall Street system for themselves. They were amassing fortunes, but their lives were all focused inward.

What a contrast to a man like Moses. At an old age he received a call that was not for himself but for others. When God called him, He said, "I have seen ... I have heard ... I am concerned ... I have come down to rescue." And then He told Moses, in effect, "You're here to work for Me." (See Exodus 3:7-10.)

And isn't that why God called Barnabas in the New Testament? We think the Apostle Paul was a great man, and he was; but how much greater was Barnabas, the man who encouraged the Apostle Paul? Barnabas was Paul's teacher and helper. There is a beautiful description of him in Acts 11:22-26. Barnabas is a model for us. We may not be like Paul, but any of us can be a Barnabas.

Scripture says, "Let us encourage one another" (Hebrews 10:25). We all have opportunity to do that. We all have an opportunity to give, to teach, and to encourage. Why else did God give the gifts of the Spirit to the church? Why did He give them to you and to me?

Ephesians 4:11 says that God gave gifts, and verse 12 tells us why, "To prepare God's people for works of service, so that the body of Christ may be built up." And in 1 Peter 4:10 we read, "Each one should use whatever gift he has received to serve others, faithfully administering God's grace in its various forms."

Why did God pour so much into us if not for others?

First Thessalonians 5:11 says, "Encourage one another and build each other up." How can we do that if we're not also learning and growing ourselves?

In his book *Racing Toward 2001*, Russell Chandler quotes a bioethics expert, Fay Angus, who said, " 'The best we can do is to exercise the depth of the wisest among us.' "[2] Well, who are the wisest, if not those who have lived long lives and are experienced, who have learned and are still learning?

Our Spiritual Assets

What am I doing with the spiritual assets God has given me? We have what so many need—precepts, concepts, and principles. Let others learn from us, then put what they learn to work in their own lives. Our task is to invest ourselves and give to others.

All over Asia many full-time missionaries are teachers of English as a second language because that's the need where they are. As I meet these teachers, they tell me that we can go as teachers too. Sometimes the teachers are paid by the government, sometimes by a university, sometimes by a private company.

"But I don't know that culture," you may say. "And I certainly don't know that language." That's right, but you know English and that's what is wanted. People in other countries who want to learn English tell us that they want to learn it from those who live in an English-speaking country, because these people won't try to translate. The learner will be immersed in English by a native speaker from the moment he enters the classroom.

And even though you may be paid to teach English as a second language, you will be a teacher of much more, because the students, the businessmen, and the mothers of young children want to know much more. In their homes, in a tearoom, or on the street you will have wonderful opportunities to tell what you believe about Jesus. Recently I visited with a teacher of English who taught in a Japanese church. She said, "We used Bible lessons in our teaching. For many this was their first exposure to a church and to Christianity."

George Hilton of Calgary, Alberta went to Ethiopia to teach what he knew best—computers. Let him tell it:

"I retired in 1982 with some computer skills. In 1991 I went to Eritrea, a province of Ethiopia. The thirty-year war had ended in May 1990, and the Canadian government was giving computers to the church in Eritrea. The church there was running a food-for-work program, and we in the Baptist Union of Western Canada were supplying the funds and food for this program through our national organization, The Sharing Way.

"But in Ethiopia they were having problems. They had set up the program to be sure that people who got food also did some work in rebuilding the country. They were keeping track of all this manually, in writing; they needed computer control. So two of us went to Eritrea. I wrote the program to control the food distribution and taught twenty-five people how to use it. We had two computers to train those twenty-five people, so we worked out a schedule of a half hour per day per person from 8:00 A.M. to 8:00 P.M. It was 10:00 P.M. before we got back to our place of residence for supper. In six weeks not one person missed his or her class time; they were eager to learn.

"It was such a rewarding experience. Their language is Tygrinia and we had to work through interpreters. I never saw such a prayerful, thankful people. They just couldn't believe that we would help them at our own expense. Today they are still using the computers and the program.

"Frankly, some things were difficult. We had a tin of drinking water for the whole day. But when we got used to it, it was fine. I find that if you use common sense you should be able to roll with this kind of thing. I'm not saying it is easy, but certainly a well-adjusted older person is better at doing this than some younger people. I think being older gives us more ability to cope with it. I only had one sick day the whole time I was there."

George Hilton was not only teaching. He also learned something—that old isn't a liability; it can be an asset.

As I age, who am I helping? In whom am I investing my time and experience? Who am I mentoring? A good mentor is a guide.

Philip was a mentor to an Ethiopian who was driving down from Jerusalem to Gaza. When Philip drew alongside, he heard the man reading Scripture. The Bible says, "He invited Philip to come up and sit with him."

When we read that text in Acts 8:31 we find that Philip began where the man was and announced, or proclaimed, Jesus. He didn't discuss politics or the environment or social issues, or some different doctrine; he began where the man was and told him about Jesus.

If we're going to start where people are, it means listening to them and hearing what they already know so that we can build on it.

Then we can help them, direct them. That's what Philip did. If we are ready to help someone, if we are ready to announce Jesus to someone, chances are good that God is ready to take us to that one. He did with Philip; He did with George Hilton. Who is God preparing for you right now?

Why Not Me?

Recently I read an article written by a seventy-five-year-old grandfather who spoke about the need to share our faith with other people. The whole article was experience after experience of the blessings of telling others about his faith in Christ, and I thought, *Why not more of us? What's keeping us back? What's stopping me?*

I think I have figured it out. I have always wondered why so many people are fearful of giving a clear witness to their faith in Christ, even when someone asks them questions about the Savior. Many folks hem and haw, hesitate, backpedal, sidestep, and I always thought it was because they felt unequipped or ill at ease or uncertain about the faith. But after reading Paul's words in 1 Corinthians 4:15, I am wondering if there is another reason. The Apostle said, "Even though you have ten thousand guardians in Christ, you do not have many fathers, for in Christ Jesus I became your father through the gospel."

In other words he is the one who brought them along to faith. But then comes the next sentence, "Therefore I urge you to imitate me." There it is. That has got to be part of the reason that too many Christians are hesitant witnesses. It is not because they are unsure of Christ or of what He has done in their lives, or even unsure of the scriptural promises. But there is a fear that the people who come to faith through their witness might seek to imitate them, to pattern their lives after them, and they know themselves so well that they are thinking, "Don't look at me. Don't depend on me. Look at Jesus, yes, but not me."

Well, why not me? If Christ lives in me, why not me? If I fall down and get up and seek forgiveness, isn't that valuable for people to see? If I make a horrible mistake but show that God is still willing to take me back, isn't that a good lesson for others to learn? We think people want to imitate our perfection, and we are not perfect. Maybe what they want to see is what Christ can do in the life of an ordinary, everyday, clay-footed Christian— someone just like us.

Do we think we will not be heard? There is great spiritual interest sweeping our world right now. Often it's confused, but there is an openness, a readiness to hear. There is an opportunity for us, particularly if we have lived a life of faith and can talk about it. In a society of cafeteria religions, people who have been faithful to Christ over the long haul will be heard.

A People for Today

We may not influence society as a whole, but we can point to the One who can change individuals one at a time. We've got the ability to do that. And isn't the ultimate measure of a fruitful Christian other Christians?

If we are not attached to the vine, we will not bear fruit; but if we are attached, then we will bear fruit because our Savior will produce it. "I am the vine; you are the branches," He said. "Remain in me. . . . Apart from me you can do nothing." But by remaining in Him, you "will bear much fruit" (John 15:4-5).

The time is right; the information we have and the life to back it up are right. We have what it takes and we are living in a time when people are now beginning to seek again what folks fifty, sixty, seventy years ago took for granted that everybody knew.

Today many people who do not know about God want to know. The Gospel may now be foreign to our culture, but in some ways it has always been foreign to every culture. If we are to weave the Gospel into our culture, that means we must understand both the Gospel and the culture to which we bring it. It means knowing where people are coming from and then speaking to them on their terms.

Commenting about the wrecks of people's lives, someone said, "They could have used a road map." They could, and we have it. People don't know the directions; they lack a reference point and are without guidelines. Didn't God place us here to be mentors and guides to such people?

More and more social scientists are discovering that personal rights separated from social responsibility are tearing us apart as a society. So many younger people have never known what most older people know: the meaning of social responsibility. People need to be taught. They need to be shown. The very act of mentoring gives us the privilege—a little here, a little there, precept by precept—to show what it means to live in society as responsible persons and particularly as committed Christians.

With God's call to the Apostle Paul came a description of evangelism that is relevant today. In Acts 26, as Paul tells King Agrippa about his conversion and his calling, he says that the Lord told him he was being sent "to open their eyes and turn them from darkness to light, and from the power of Satan to God, so that they may receive forgiveness of sins and a place among those who are sanctified by faith in me" (Acts 26:18).

There is the pattern for us. There is the whole of evangelism. The message of redemption is to open people's eyes so that they may turn from darkness to light, from the dominion of Satan to God, and receive forgiveness of sins and an inheritance among those who have been sanctified by faith in the Lord Jesus.

If you forget the steps, turn to Acts 26:18 and read them again. Check yourself when you talk to another person about salvation. You will realize what God is doing. You will understand why He is doing it. And you will see what happens when our Lord touches a person's life.

Many people know something about Christianity and the Bible, but they don't know all they should know, and we have an obligation to teach them.

Apollos was like that. We read that "Apollos, a native of Alexandria, came to Ephesus. He was a learned man, with a thorough knowledge of the Scriptures" (Acts 18:24). He "had been instructed in the way of the Lord, and he spoke with great fervor and taught about Jesus accurately" (v. 25). What he knew, he knew well, but "he knew only the baptism of John" (v. 25). There was more for him to know.

How did he learn? God used a husband and wife team, Priscilla and Aquila. When they heard him teaching, they didn't contradict him. As far as it went, his teaching was accurate. Rather, "they invited him to their home, and explained to him the way of God more adequately" (Acts 18:26). He still had more to learn. These coteachers helped him.

I remember when, as a new believer knowing a little bit, I was teaching and even preaching. A husband and wife team took me aside more than once and added to what I knew. They did not tell me to be quiet until I knew more. They encouraged me as a teacher and preacher. They added to my biblical understanding. That's what Priscilla and Aquila did.

I am glad for people who will encourage others, never

putting them down but helping them build on what they already know. That's a real contribution to the Christian church, and something you and I can do even when we become physically too old to still be preachers and teachers ourselves.

No Phony Talk

Every generation is a new mission field. We were the mission field for somebody ahead of us. Now others are the mission field for us. People today are turned off by phony talk and advertising hype; they want something genuine. They want to hear from people who won't lie to them. They don't want to know about denominations and they don't want to know about Christianity as a religion; they want to know about Christ.

I remember on a particular trip to Israel visiting with a man who was explaining to me something that had happened in biblical history. Suddenly he turned to me and asked, "Are you a Christian?" I replied, "Yes, I am." He came right back with, "Are you a believing Christian?" I knew what he meant. Of course, there is no such thing as an unbelieving Christian, but he wanted to get beyond labels. He wanted to know, "Are you a believing Christian?" And that's what our culture is asking us. They want to get past the phonies, the charlatans, the hypocrites, the people who make the negative newspaper stories. "Are you a believing Christian?" If you are, you've got something to teach.

Don't Worry about the Church

A telephone call came late one evening. The man on the line wanted to talk. He was concerned about some shady dealings on the part of Christians. What should he do? How should he handle it?

We talked about God's church. We talked about weaknesses and failures, and about our responsibility to examine our own lives before God. And, based on Scripture and experience, I was able to assure him that God knows His church very well. God loves the church. He is not blind to people's faults and He will cleanse the church.

We are never to give in to the unethical or the improper. Even though it may seem that others are getting away with something, really they are not. Then I reminded this caller that the New Testament Epistles were written because there were problems in the church. It wasn't all that it was supposed to be then and it isn't now. God will work on His church.

Peter wrote, "Dear friends, I urge you, as aliens and strangers in the world, to abstain from sinful desires, which war against your soul" (1 Peter 2:11). We are in a corrupt world that will lead us down wrong paths if we let it. What happens then will war against our souls. We are to be on guard.

My friend's problems are still there, and he still has to work and live in the midst of them. But God dealt with problems in the church in the past, and He will deal with them now.

Most people don't know what it is to follow Jesus. They have nothing in society, nothing in the media, that can guide them. And sometimes they are turned off by the church. They don't know what following Christ means; they haven't seen it. You may be God's teacher sent to someone who wants to know. I remember listening to a man give an example of this. He told of a friend who was converted but who continued to live with his girlfriend. Finally someone kindly showed this new Christian what the Bible says about such a relationship. "Oh," he said, "I didn't know." His conscience couldn't be his guide. Until then, his conscience had been influenced by the culture around him. A simple word, an explanation from Scripture, and he was set on the right path.

Somebody once said, "Don't yell at culture. Don't fight it. Recognize it and go out into it." He used the illustration of the weather. We check out the weather and we dress accordingly. We check out people to whom we're ministering, we prepare accordingly, and then we go, in the love of God.

Ready to Fail; Ready to Succeed

One of the toughest things I ever faced when I became a new believer was the recognition that Christ did not mean the same to others that He meant to me. In my excitement about having met Jesus Christ as my Savior and Lord, I wanted to tell others the Good News. How painful it was for me when, after listening to the message of salvation, a friend turned to me and said, "No."

The Apostle Paul knew something of that and quoted Scripture itself when he wrote, "All day long I have held out my hands to a disobedient and obstinate people" (Romans 10:21). That's God talking. "All day long." There's no time when God's hands are not outstretched, no time when He stops saying, "Come unto Me," no time when His love for us lessens. "All day long I have held out my hands to a disobedient and obstinate people."

It's one thing for people who do not know that God loves them, who do not know how to respond, to go through life without the Savior. But for people who do know God loves them, who do know why Jesus Christ went to the cross, who do understand that He rose from the dead to give life eternal—for those people to say, "No, I won't" is painful. They are disobedient and obstinate. Such people are all around us, in our families and in our neighborhoods. We know them by name and we love them. How much more God loves them. They need us to teach them.

In mentoring, teaching, and helping, will you be hurt? Yes, you will. Those you help the most may hurt you the most. I remember helping a young man through a prison ministry. He trusted the Savior. When he was released, he came to us because he had nowhere else to go. He even lived with us until he got on his feet. We found him a job; in time he married. Then one day he turned on me. To him I had become an enemy. I did not understand it then, nor do I now. But that's a risk we take in mentoring, helping.

Fortunately, the opposite experience is more frequent. One day my phone rang and the man on the other end gave his name, then paused. "Don't you remember me?" he asked. I had to confess that I did not. Then he told me, "Thirty-three years ago in Philadelphia you brought me along to faith in Christ." What a happy visit we had as he told me how he continues on with Christ today.

Many hurting people are also broken; your help won't necessarily be welcomed. You may not be a counselor or medical practitioner, but you are a friend. You teach as a friend, but you have to be ready to be rejected as well.

Maturity is our ally. Having the advantage of age is a wonderful asset. It gives us a philosophical view that "this too will change." We already know how years can make a difference in what is happening in a person's life. We have heard almost all the problems before. We listen to each person carefully because it is new and overwhelming to him, but it isn't new to us. We listen, we turn to God's Word, and we pray.

As a mentor and teacher, you will meet those who have been spiritually injured. You will meet some who have philosophical questions, many who are angry or bitter, and others who are oppressed by demons. But God gives help through His Word for all of these. Be sure you are getting alone with God and His Word, praying and being nurtured yourself. Be sure you are seeking others who can mentor you. Keep on learning so that you are giving from an overflowing cup.

Help One or Help Millions

I know a writer who reaches millions of people with her words. But there is something about her success that not many know. She turns for counsel, encouragement, and prayer to a couple in their eighties. She pours out her heart to them. They listen, ask questions, and make suggestions. Most of all, they pray—with her and for her. She leaves their home with a new sense of direction, encouraged to go back to her computer. Who has the greater ministry, this writer who reaches millions through her books or the couple in their eighties who counsel and pray for her?

One day as I was cutting my grass, I thought of Adam and Eve. Poor Adam and Eve—what a responsibility they had. They didn't just have to keep the grass cut and the weeds down in one yard. Adam and Eve were given the job of taking care of the whole earth. "God blessed them and said to them, 'Be fruitful and increase in number; fill the earth and subdue it. Rule over the fish of the

sea and the birds of the air and over every living crea-
ture that moves on the ground' " (Genesis 1:28).

But just as we can make a yard beautiful, we can help
make people beautiful too. God will bring to us men and
women and young people who need what God has already given to us. Our remaining time on earth can
leave people better off for our having been here. Someday what we teach them will be passed along by them to
still one more person. And, after all, isn't that why we
continue to be pupils and teachers?

For Reflection:

1. Who are you pouring your life into right now?

2. What new things have you been learning this year to
make yourself better able to teach?

3. Who is helping you to stretch and grow? What new
opportunities for learning are you seeking?

4. What are you doing right now, today, with the spiritual assets God has given you?

5. God's hands are outstretched to _____ [name].
Will you be God's Good News messenger to that person?

Come Snuggle with Me

5

"Some people, no matter how old they get, never lose their beauty. They merely move it from their faces into their hearts."
Author unknown

"People living deeply have no fear of death."
Anaïs Nin

In my local newspaper I read a story about Grand-friends. These are people who are giving themselves to children and, oh, what a difference they make. A grand-friend who never had children of her own says, "When someone tells me the effect I've had on a child I've worked with, I can hardly believe it."

These men and women, all seniors, all retired, volunteer their services at schools, day-care centers, and family provider homes. They read stories and talk. One grandfriend says, "This little girl and I just sit and visit and visit. I think we could sit all day and talk. All you need to do is just talk with them. You don't need to reprimand them or anything like that."

Some grandfriends work with babies. "Our children need a lot of holding, cuddling, and playing," said one family care provider. "Some just rock and feed the babies."

Not every grandfriend who volunteers is mobile. Some are homebound, but that doesn't stop them from giving themselves to children. A coordinator of Telefriends said that this program "connects older adult volunteers with children who are either home alone after school or who could use some extra attention and support from an adult." Then she added, "A lot of our volunteers are from nursing homes; they can't get out but they can still get involved by phone."

These are the people who have learned the value of snuggling.

Kids Are Scared

Have you listened to children lately? They are scared. Ask a child what he wants to be when he grows up and he might answer you, "*If* I grow up." They're afraid of being shot or kidnapped or hurt in some way. They know others, in their school, on their street, who have been abducted or killed. This is a fear most of us never had to face when we were children. Are they safe in their homes? Not if a stray bullet comes through the window, and they know other kids who have been shot in their own homes.

Some senior adults bewail the changes in our society. "Why can't kids behave as we did when we were younger? What's wrong with our society?" These older people barricade themselves inside their homes, or flee to other places to get away; in so doing they separate themselves from an opportunity to say to a child, "Come snuggle with me." Or, an opportunity to say to a teenager, "Let's talk." Or, an opportunity to say to a single mom or dad who is trying to cope with a job and children and finances, "How can I help?"

God will direct people who are ready to help to those who are needy. God has placed us in a position where we can be responsive. We are the right age; we are available; we are safe. Doesn't God have a right to believe that we will be responsive? Olena Mae Welsh discovered that she had something to offer people with needs.

"I work at College Church in Wheaton, Illinois with a special education program for persons who are disabled. We don't limit it to College Church members, but open it to other communities and churches as well. We have Sunday morning worship services with Bible school classes for them. Two Friday nights a month we have a dinner and devotions. We also have a camping program, a music program, and a parents' support group.

"My main responsibility is with the parents. I find it very fulfilling and rewarding. It is a ministry reaching out with the love of Christ to hurting families.

"My husband passed away twelve years ago. He had been chaplain and then alumni chaplain at Wheaton College for twenty-six years. When he died, I had to find something to do. This position was offered to me even though I never had handicapped children of my own. So I tried to learn with the job. The Lord has blessed and I'm thankful.

"I had been so active in ministry with my husband. Then to have nothing was a bit devastating. I'm seventy-four now and hoping to go to at least seventy-five, maybe beyond that.

"It is wearing at times, but I love it. I find it so satisfying. The parents are excited that this is available because not many churches provide this type of program."

Accepting Our Opportunities

Caring, loving, and snuggling start with thinking of ourselves as friends and then accepting the opportunities that God brings to us. Who's available? Who is not shocked by substance abuse or pornography or lack of moral values? People with a lot of seasons behind them. Mature Christian adults understand that they must take people where they are and minister to them.

We have an opportunity for ministry that perhaps has never been quite so needed before. Oh, there are still old-fashioned adults who think that anyone younger than themselves ought to follow the principles and behavior patterns that existed fifty years ago. There are still self-centered older people who think that others should be interested in them, when they don't even know the names or ages of their neighbor children. But not all. There are thinking, mature adults who understand that we have to take our society as we find it; this is the mission field God has given us. The need is all around.

Not long ago a poll revealed that what teenagers fear most is the breakup of their family through divorce or death. They want the security of a home, but they don't all have that. We can't make a child's home different, but we can become a friend, a spiritual helper, and make a difference to that child. Have you thought about it? To whom will you be family when that person's real family is coming apart?

The fact that many families are damaged and dysfunctional is not news. Illegitimacy and divorce are leading even secular writers to say, "Our children are in worse shape than we thought."

We live in a time of social confusion. A newspaper headline read, "One in fifty under age fifteen may have a jailed parent." Who's going to be family to those children? Another headline read, "Boy, eleven years of age, sues parents for divorce."

"But I can't help them," you say, "and certainly I can't help them as a Christian; they're not interested in what I believe." That's not true. Many are very interested. Not only young people but their parents are in a fluid state religiously. They're open, they're searching, they're going in many different directions to find meaning for their lives. We live in an age of spiritual hunger. It is not a Christian age—far from it—but it is a searching age; and whether a person is sixteen or thirty-six, chances are he or she has not formed religious convictions but is open to discussing questions with someone secure enough to hear them.

They Need a Family

We are told that by the turn of the century as many as half of all American adults will be single. Who will they have for family? Who will they talk to? Who will listen to them and hear their concerns? Who will provide care for their children? Who will be a comfort to mothers or fathers trying to cope on their own, who don't know what to do in the face of illness, who don't have a parent or a grandparent to turn to? Those who are so far away from their extended family through moves, job changes, or just estranged relationships that they don't know whom to ask for help when a child has a fever or they're experiencing troubles of their own? Who has the years of wisdom to offer and the time? You do. I do.

I have met young people who seem to despise themselves. They don't say that, but they act out their feelings of worthlessness. Sometimes that attitude works itself out through defensiveness, a sharp tongue, disobedience, even through criminal behavior. But it comes down to, "I don't like me. Therefore, nobody else could like me either." Did God place us nearby to like them?

The Apostle Paul wrote to Timothy, "Don't let anyone look down on you because you are young, but set an example for the believers in speech, in life, in love, in faith and in purity" (1 Timothy 4:12). One of the worst things an older person can do is to accept at face value the despising of a young person for himself and then reflect it back. "Don't let anyone look down on you because you are young," Paul said, "but set an example for the believers in speech, in life, in love, in faith and in purity." We can help young people do that.

Attitudes dictate behavior. Behavior reflects attitudes. God doesn't despise anybody. God's people, if they are obedient, don't despise anybody either. One of the best things we can do for young people is to let them know in every way, "Look what you are worth to me! Look what you are worth to God!"

Who Has Security? Who Has Peace?

No matter where people look, no matter what they plan on or hope for, they don't find much that will make them secure. They often can't even depend on the words and promises of other people.

We can't be silent or retreat into ourselves at a time when people are searching for answers. All around us are people with needs who don't have our spiritual resources, people who are insecure physically, emotionally, and financially.

The words of Jesus come to us in times like these, and then reach to others, "I tell you the truth, whoever hears my word and believes him who sent me has eternal life and will not be condemned; he has crossed over from death to life" (John 5:24).

Have you crossed over from death to life? If you have, then everything else becomes secondary—pleasure, security, even peace. You have life. You don't have to fear anymore. Our Lord said: "Whoever hears my word and believes him who sent me...." If you have heard and believed it, if you are trusting what He said, then you have crossed over from having nothing to offer to having everything to offer. You have so much to give others because you have life.

When nothing else is certain, the words of Jesus are certain. When nothing else is true, this is true. "I tell you the truth," our Lord said. We can believe it, we can entrust our lives to it, we can launch out in our final years of life with a giving love that grows out of it.

Recently our daughter's car was hit from behind. The impact was so hard that it sent her eighty-four feet onto a grassy median. Now she has back problems that we hope can be corrected. The driver of the other car had neither insurance nor a valid license. He was not supposed to be driving.

Why do such things happen? We know that we cannot plan our days. We have to be ready for any emergency or surprise. In his very practical book James tells us, "Now listen, you who say, 'Today or tomorrow we will go to this or that city, spend a year there, carry on business and make money.' Why, you do not even know what will happen tomorrow. What is your life? You are a mist that appears for a little while and then vanishes" (James 4:13-14).

We don't know what tomorrow is going to bring. We don't even know what today is going to bring. We could pull up to a traffic light, be waiting for it to change, and suddenly somebody from behind could hit us. My daughter thought her day was starting out like any other. In just an instant she had a wrecked car. Worse, she had an injured back. None of us can plan. We can only trust God to carry us through. We aren't prepared for life because we have every detail planned out. We are prepared for life, and prepared to help others, because we belong to the Living Christ who knows exactly where we are and what is happening to us. When so many around us are being battered from one direction or another, we are prepared to offer help.

Is my home, my single room, or my apartment, a place where people can come and be renewed and helped and encouraged? Do I need great strength to do that? Do I need a vast education to do that? I have life's resources because I have walked with Christ and I can draw on that. So can you.

When someone finds us to be a friend they can turn to, we can open the Scriptures and say, "Let me show you what God says." We draw from our own security in Christ so that we can put our arms around an adult or a child and say, "Why don't we give this to God?" and give them exposure to an experience with God through prayer that they may never have had before. We offer the peace that people need. From our home, even in a nursing home, we offer security, not rancor, not more confusion, not more pain, not more attacks. People get that all the time. With us they will find a difference. They will know where to go for help.

"But what about me? I still have needs too." The psalmist thought about that, and he wrote: "Cast your cares on the Lord and he will sustain you; he will never let the righteous fall" (Psalm 55:22). I am interested that he did not say, "Cast your cares on the Lord and he will take them away," or, "Life will be smooth and pleasant and comfortable and happy and convenient." He said, "Cast your cares on the Lord and he will sustain you."

The cares will be in God's hands. He will sustain you through those cares. He will understand every part of them, and He will be your sustaining power.

So it comes down to each one of us saying, "My cares are going to be there because I am living in a world that creates all kinds of problems for me. Do I want to face those problems and cares on my own? Or do I want to face those problems and cares with God who promises to sustain me?" When we grasp that, we will be able to say to others, "I understand; I've been there. Come snuggle with me."

Who Cares? About You, about Others?

We don't have to go far away to have a ministry to others. And it doesn't have to be dramatic. It might be as quiet as a ministry of prayer.

George Stokes, a former professor at Baylor University, has learned that. He says, "Some go all over the world. I'm still here at home. We have got to serve at whatever level we can. The best thing we can do is to stay steady and be dependable in our local church. We've tried always to be available to do whatever our local church wanted us to do.

"I've never been on an overseas trip. I've given most of my life week by week to the local church. It's not dramatic, but it is essential to the Christian faith.

"I keep a written prayer list. Sometimes it takes the first forty minutes of the day just to get through the list. I've had as many as a hundred on the list in years past.

"The fact that a person takes time to talk to God about another person does the person praying as much good as the one being prayed for. You'll never see my name in lights, but I'll still be in my chair praying." There's a man who understands his worth to others!

Before I became a believer in Christ, I tried handling my cares by myself—it didn't work! It never does, but many people don't know that. They don't know how to deal with their fears—whether they are ten years old, twenty years old, or forty years old. We who know can help them.

I admit that I sometimes argue with Scripture, especially when I read a verse like Proverbs 1:33, "But whoever listens to me will live in safety and be at ease, without fear of harm." And I find myself saying, "Wait a minute. I believe in God. I trust Him. But I can't say that I'm quiet from fear.

"I can't say that I always sense that I dwell safely." But then I look at the verse again, "But whoever *listens* to me will live in safety and be at ease, without fear of harm." "Listens to me" means "being alert to, giving respectful attention to."

We all want to be quiet from fear. We all want to dwell in safety. Well, who knows how to take care of us best? God does! Who knows what causes fear in our lives? God does! Who knows how to make us dwell safely? God does. If you are like me and want the last part of that verse—dwelling safely, being quiet from fear—then you had better learn the first part, and that is to give respectful attention to God.

We're Different; So Are They

We who are senior adults are not going to grow older the same way our parents did. God knew that when we were born and when He permitted our life experiences, whether pain, hardship, trials, or joys. God has always known how to help us come through victoriously on the other side. God knows everything there is to know about our culture and our neighborhoods. God knows where we are and what we are facing at a time when people need what we have to offer. We aren't going to be like older people were before; young people aren't like the young used to be either.

Recently I read about a grandmother in Toronto befriending street kids. Seventy-four years old, and she cares about street kids! She's well dressed; they're grubby. She's articulate; they're often school dropouts. She's optimistic; they're disillusioned. But she's their "grandma." She says she has a head start—the years between her and those she ministers to gives her the advantage of reaching out in love, of being grandma to them. She's not a threat. She says she is no one special, but she is there for them. And that's what the kids say too.

Who can say about you, "She is there for me"? "He is there for me"? Children are often thought to have little value. Parents struggling on their own often feel that they have little value, especially if they've already been rejected through divorce. Who will put their arms around these people and say, "I'm here for you"? Often the best person is a nonthreatening, loving senior adult.

God Is Ready If You Are

Are you praying about this? The Holy Spirit will lead you if you are. You may say, "I don't know anybody."

Do you want to be useful to the kingdom? Do you want to be that resource for someone who thinks, "I can't face what I'm going through"? Will that person discover someone older who is interested in where people are right now? Will that person discover you?

In an interview one teenager said, "We all want to be loved. We all want someone to show us that we're worth something. We all want to have a pat on the back for what we've done well."

"Isn't there anybody who will do that for me?" young people ask. "My parents? They are always gone." Or, "My parents are split up. On the streets I'm used. Will you listen to me?"

Kent Boothman and his wife, Marie, who live in Edmonds, Washington, have been missionaries; now they want to work in the troubled inner city.

After spending five years in Africa, Kent Boothman went back to his insurance business. But he had learned about ministry. "We've changed focus. For five years we were in Conakry, Guinea, Africa. Marie started a guest house and took care of missionaries and visitors coming into the country, about 200 guests per month. I was the business administrator for the Christian and Missionary Alliance and the government contact person for all Protestant missionaries.

"Other retirees could do this, but they would have to be flexible. We did well in Africa because we caught on to the language, people, and customs. I was the pastor of the international church, an English-speaking African church. We built it up enough to call a full-time African pastor. I also worked with relief organizations.

"We'd like to retire about age sixty, but we spent everything we had going to Africa, so we have to start over financially.

"We love Africa and had a wonderful ministry there. Now we are working in the inner city, trying to mesh job and ministry.

"The American church seems to have really turned inward. Lots of talk about 'what's wrong with me.' You're not going to get involved in ministry if you have that perspective; you're too busy looking at yourself. I would say to someone getting ready to retire and waiting to take it easy, 'You are at a crossroads and you are missing the sweetness of life.'

"We are going to move to the inner city. We want to buy a house there and eventually have a safe house for people.

"Before we went to Africa, Marie had a street ministry with women whose husbands were in prison. One of them had two little kids. That woman had left home when she was fourteen and lived seven years in a car. Today she is a computer programmer, living with her husband who is out of prison and going straight. Marie worked with her, taught her, started a housekeeping company and hired her and other women to get them off welfare. Most people need a jump-start. They need ideas about what to do.

"I found that if you have a ministry goal you have a better attitude toward living for the future."

Someone to Trust

In a survey taken not long ago, one third of all Americans said you can't trust anyone other than perhaps your closest family, and sometimes not them. But I know trustworthy older adults who have no ax to grind, nothing to gain, but a lot of love to give. And love will always draw people. Light always attracts. Where do we get the resources? Our resource is in the Living Lord Christ. We are growing in Him and He gives us the love we need for others.

The majority of people don't understand the Christian faith. They're not even sure they understand religion. They get a little New Age, a little Eastern mysticism, a potpourri of this and that. We live in a time of supermarket religion, a cafeteria style of selecting this and that with no standards beyond our own. Who will explain what it is to trust the Savior? Who will explain what it means to place our faith in Jesus Christ? Who will explain the crucifixion and the resurrection and the second coming of Christ? This is new to people who have never had any religious experience.

Thousands of young people today have never seen a Bible, never heard a Bible story, don't know who God is, and don't know Jesus beyond a curse word. We don't have to be trained theologians to explain to them the simplicities of faith and to plant seeds of understanding. If you are their shelter in a storm, they are already attentive, listening, wondering what it is that you have that they don't. When we read in the Bible about the Good Samaritan, we recognize that what he gave was time and money and concern. You may not have money, but you have time and concern. Are you a Good Samaritan? Can our Lord bring someone across your path, someone who is beaten up emotionally, somebody who is battered spiritually? Will you help that person?

Will you be a nurturer, even if no one else in the community is? Will you help young people and adults understand what it means to think Christianly, to apply biblical teachings to their lives? To see that God cares about schoolwork, about job promotions, about divorces, about battered children, about finances? Will you expose

Christian thinking to these areas? Or will you only complain that most adults and young people don't know
how to think Christianly? How can they, unless someone shows them?

Thinking Christianly isn't an opinion. It isn't simply
what you think or I think. Rather, it's a matter of "Your
attitude should be the same as that of Christ Jesus" (Philippians 2:5). And if you are a person of the Book,
grounded in Scripture, who this very day spent time
with God in prayer, you are ready for that someone
whom God could bring across your path.

A Sense of History, a Need to Belong

Young people are asking, "Who will care for me? Should
I join a gang? Is that the only family there is for me? Are
there no alternatives?" As one rock song puts it, "I can't
get any lower; still, I feel that I'm sinking." Many teenagers say that religion is very important to them. In fact,
religion frightens them because they don't know enough
about it. And what little bit they know makes them feel
that they're guilty before God. Surveys taken among
young people show that many of Protestant background
are very interested in Roman Catholicism. Why? It is not
so much for the teachings, not for the rules, but rather
for a sense of history, a sense of belonging. You and I
can offer belonging. We can offer warmth. In Christ we
can offer that sense of history.

Even with college students there is opportunity for us
to help. The *Christian Century* recently reported, "These
are not people yearning to be left alone by adults.
... Today's students do not seem obsessed by the search
for freedom. They seem much more interested in the
search for roots, stability, order, and identity."[1]

Dr. Michael Green, who now serves as Advisor in Evangelism to the Archbishops of Canterbury and York, once said that the church itself is part of the Gospel. It's part of communicating the Gospel. And he's right. We are the Gospel; we are being read. We are the church; we are being seen.

So Much to Give Away

Look at all we have to give away to others—all that God has lavished on us. To be a family to those living alone, to those raising children alone, to children who may have many grandparents and step-grandparents but none who care for them.

Lavished—did you know that word is in the Bible? Paul writes about God's grace which He freely bestowed on us, and he goes on to say, "In him we have redemption through his blood, the forgiveness of sins, in accordance with the riches of God's grace that he lavished on us with all wisdom and understanding" (Ephesians 1:7-8). He freely bestowed the riches of His grace. He lavished them upon us.

How much more could we want? His riches—not just freely given but lavished upon us. And if we're that rich with His grace, His unmerited favor, His gifts, what could we possibly lack?

Shut your eyes and picture it ... not just a free pouring out of His grace upon us but a lavishing of God's grace. And if so much has been lavished on us, can we hold back when we see the needs of others?

We hear of children who don't know who they belong to. The husband of their mother is not their father, nor was the husband of a few years ago their father. And their own father is someplace else. They are longing for roots. Can you help people who are rootless, who know nothing of the security that you have now and probably had in your own childhood? Can you spiritually adopt those who need you so much?

Many people say that family is anything you want it to be: you can be single and have a family; you can be homosexual and have a family; even a gang is considered by some to be a family. People long for true family, and we can become that for someone. It takes no special gift or training to do it. We just need to be ready to give ourselves away.

I meet people from time to time who like to talk the Gospel but don't necessarily want to live the Gospel. I meet people who place a wall between themselves and others. They sort of throw the Gospel message over the wall but don't want to go around the wall to relate to people.

The Apostle Paul knew better. He told the church in Thessalonica, "We loved you so much that we were delighted to share with you not only the gospel of God but our lives as well, because you had become so dear to us" (1 Thessalonians 2:8). People read the Gospel through the person presenting it. If the life doesn't bear out what is being said, then people ask, "What is the value? How does this apply to me?" But when somebody gives himself, makes a present of his life to Christ and involves himself with people—caring for them, encouraging and helping them—then when he talks about the Lord Jesus Christ, he has a message people want to hear.

Can you say with the Apostle Paul, "We were delighted to share with you not only the gospel of God but our lives as well"? If you are good with the one but not so good with the other, maybe it is time to pray about that and then do something about it.

We Are Repair People for Broken Lives

A senior high school teacher discussing the difference between teaching now and some years ago said, "We spend so much time now repairing broken lives, trying to help kids who come to school after having been up late at night because there has been shouting and fighting or drugs in the home and they cannot study, they cannot sleep. Or they may have to work to earn money for food because there's no food in the house; a lot of young people tell us today that they are the providers of the family food as well as for their own needs such as clothing.

"How do you teach them when they're tired, hungry, and feeling emotionally battered?" this teacher asked. "When educators lament the drop in test scores and blame the schools, they may have overlooked another factor, that some teachers can't even get to their subjects because they're doing so much repair work."

And if it's true at the senior high level, it's true at the beginning levels as well. A primary school teacher said, "I teach remedial education to children who failed kindergarten. They haven't learned their colors, they can't print their name, they don't know their address." Then she said, "These kids can't function in school but they're so street-wise. They may be little, but in street wisdom they're seventeen." This teacher added, "One of the problems we face with these children who failed kindergarten is that among other things some of them are already sexually active." Who's going to care for them? What kind of start are they getting?

Do we have a relationship with a loving Father? Can we pass that along to these children? Can we be family to others, regardless of how old we are? Can we offer togetherness? Where else can a single mom find a mother to give counsel? Where else can a young man find an older man who will listen to him and talk to him as a father or grandfather? Who doesn't yearn for a grandfather to talk to or a grandmother to hug?

Many singles live alone in apartments. Subdivisions of young families often don't communicate. Even older people in senior citizen high-rises don't communicate unless someone purposely reaches out. Who better than the older Christian woman to give a high five to a six-year-old who did something special in school? Who better than a "grandpa" to pick up a crying child and hold that child on his lap and read a story?

We're in a day of interactive television, but that won't satisfy the need for a listening ear. We can flip TV channels and watch videos. We can order any film we want to see. We can be exposed to anything and everything and still be lonely in the process. "Who is really there for me?" people are wondering.

Just to be prayed for by name in an understanding way is a new experience for many. There is a longing for the personal, for someone who cares, someone to stand alongside of, just as our Lord stands alongside us. Lonely people confess to wanting someone to "care about me" and "help me." We have the opportunity to do that.

Our Time to Snuggle

Don't wait for a better opportunity. This is it. "Therefore, as we have opportunity, let us do good to all people, especially to those who belong to the family of believers" (Galatians 6:10). You may not always have the opportunity to do good, so don't postpone it. If there is love to be given, give it. If there is financial help, give it. If counsel and guidance or encouragement, give it. If teaching or even correction, don't wait.

And do good to everybody—your neighbor, the person who sells you your groceries, the one who does repairs at your house, a child's teacher, the nurse at your doctor's office, the person who drives the bus—all are people to whom you can do good. Be alert to your opportunities. Wherever you go, think, "Now I have an opportunity to do good."

When we look around us at the spiritual darkness in our schools and our businesses and our country and the world, we tend to lament that there's not more spiritual light—as if somehow there just ought to be.

But we have the light of Christ to offer. That is, we do if we have come by faith to the One who is the light of the world. It is our responsibility to carry that light into the darkness around us. Some of us spend so much time crying about the terrible darkness that we forget that darkness is to be expected. Don't be surprised by it. Don't cry out in anger at the darkness. Be a bringer of light. That's our calling. We can begin right where we are. It's dark enough right there.

One day a middle-aged man told me who had made the greatest impact on his life. It was a shoe repairman who lived in his town when he was a little boy. Mr. Coffman didn't just repair shoes. He was a listener to everyone, especially to children. He had time for them when they came by his shop to talk. After he retired, Mr. Coffman was a listener then too. He might be sharpening a saw, but he had time to listen. He might be standing by his car, but he didn't just drive off; he had time to listen.

Mr. Coffman never went to college, he wasn't counted

as a world leader, but he had a lot of love. Mr. Coffman had time for people—little boys and grownups too.

He lived many years after he retired. Always he was available. Always he listened. I know how much he helped me when I was a young preacher in that West Virginia town. He listened to me too, then offered sage, biblical advice. Maybe someday, someone will remember you and me the way my friend and I remember Mr. Coffman.

Mr. Coffman knew how to snuggle.

For Reflection:

1. Have you a prayer list of people with needs? How are you putting feet on your prayers?

2. Who in your neighborhood knows you well enough to "snuggle" with you?

3. Are you training yourself to be a listener first, then an encourager? How are you doing that?

4. Think of the children and teenagers you know. Do they have your phone number? Can they call you when they want love and advice?

5. Think back to the "Mr. Coffman" in your life. Who will remember you that way?

A Friend to My Children

6

"Children begin by loving their parents. As they grow older they judge them; sometimes they forgive them."
Oscar Wilde

"Old age is but older children."
Lewis Carroll

Carefully he unwrapped the present. Then, opening a smaller box within, he took out the bronze medal and held it in his hands. I was pleased.

I was giving our son what my mother had once given me, following the death of my dad. The medal was an award from an oratorical contest my dad had won in high school more than seventy years before.

Also inside the package was a typed copy of the speech itself, about the merits of constitutional government. It was a piece of family history that I was now passing along. We cherish such moments when we can give our children gifts beyond measurable value.

Some parents, unfortunately, are not able to give gifts to their children because they haven't spoken to them in years. For them, just thinking about their loss is painful.

But for others, growing older with grown children nearby is a comfort, a pleasure, and a joy. For them, children equal contentment.

It is a simple but true statement, "Once a parent, always a parent." We never forget our children. They may be miles away. We love them, care about them, and pray for them. They may be close by, even living with us. We rejoice in their accomplishments, cry with them in their pain, pray for them in their struggles, encourage them, and realize that they are not perfect. But we are not perfect either. We never were.

Most of us say we are much wiser now than we were when our children were young. We have read books we wish had been written when we were rearing our children. We've had conversations with teachers and other professionals we wish we'd had years before. We can see the outcome of decisions that shouldn't have been made and the results of not making other decisions. We tell ourselves that we should have, could have, might have. The fact is, we didn't. We think we could have given our children more, but then honesty forces us to realize that in those days we didn't have the resources. We wish we had spent more time reading to our children, cuddling them, listening to their problems, and being available to them. But that's easier to think about now, when we don't remember quite as vividly arriving home at the end of a day worn out, stressed by problems in the workplace, to be confronted by squabbling children when what we wanted at that moment was peace. We forget what it was like as a young mom to be with them—demanding, pulling at us all day long—when we were wishing only to be able to get away for a little while and talk with another adult.

We Were Not Perfect

We were not perfect parents. No parent is. The fact is that we were both good and bad parents—depending on the day, on the circumstances, on how we felt, and on what we were facing at the moment.

Friends tell us about their own children's tragedies and we realize that we are fortunate indeed. The pain they carry is not at all like the minor nuisances that bother us. Other parents help to put things in perspective for us. Without that balance, we might look only at our failures.

With balance we realize that God is working in our children's lives now and always has been, even quite apart from us, just as He often worked in us quite apart from our parents. We hear of parents who were absolute failures, creating tragically dysfunctional families, and yet their children turn out to be strong and able and spiritually mature, in spite of their upbringing. We recognize again that the hand of God is not shortened. But we also agonize over children who are not walking with the Lord, even though they grew up knowing the truth of the Gospel. Fortunately we learn of men and women who come to faith in their thirties, forties, fifties, or sixties. God, the wonderful pursuing One, does not give up on them.

We have all seen it and it is painful to watch—a young person trying to establish his independence takes so many wrong turns. He rejects not only his mother and father as persons, but sometimes all that his mother and father taught him, including what they taught him about

God. He isn't mature enough to realize that he can stand on his own two feet and still gain from the instruction of his parents. He thinks that rejection of the parts requires rejection of the whole.

Proverbs 13:1 says, "A wise son heeds his father's instruction, but a mocker does not listen to rebuke." There are many parents who watch as a child rejects God, when what he is really doing is saying to his parents, "I'm different than you are." Not realizing his need for God, he doesn't listen to correction or instruction or rebuke. He doesn't heed his father's instruction; he doesn't take the good that his mother offers.

God gives children parents for instruction. To reject that is to reject the instruction of God. An immature person keeps saying, "Look how grown-up I am. I can do this all by myself." But a mature person says, "There is a lot of wisdom to be gained from my parents and especially from God. I'm going to heed it."

A Lot of Peace

We toss and we turn. At night we cry about our children, about some hurt that has come, a hurt that we should have let go of long ago. But we are feeling sorry for ourselves when we could have given it to God, pressed on, found victory, and come back to our children with outstretched arms to say, "This is a new day and we are new people."

The writer of the Psalms has a wonderful way of putting things together. He knows about life. Because he was inspired by God, he particularly understands my life, and yours too. Psalm 56 tells of people who have evil intentions. "They conspire, they lurk, they watch my steps, eager to take my life" (v. 6). He is talking about people who cause him problems. But he ties that together with verse 8 and says, "Record my lament; list my tears on your scroll—are they not in your record?"

Do you have tossings? At night you can't sleep? You are fretting? Most of the time it's because your child seems to have a desire to hurt, and the person he or she hurts most is you.

"Record my lament," the psalmist says. "List my tears on your scroll—are they not in your record?" And I picture God counting each one of my tears. I picture Him with a book in which He has recorded every tear and the reason for that tear. So, with the psalmist, I see on the one hand the pain and the people who cause that pain, but I see on the other hand the way God understands our pain. He has those tears recorded in His book.

Why is this important? Because God has a record, I don't have to keep a record of hurts, or supposed wrongs. There are people who rehearse old differences and open old wounds. They hurt their children and they hurt themselves, over and over again.

I can let go of hurt. I can start anew and give myself one more time to those I love—not cherishing old hurts but cherishing new beginnings. Doing that is biblical and it gives me what God gave the psalmist—a lot of peace.

There are adult children who will not hear. Some of them may never hear. That's not a measure of our faithfulness but an indication of their selective refusal, a filtering out of what we believe, especially about God. We hurt for them and what they are missing. We see the loss, not just for eternity but for the full potential of life lived in Christ right now with direction and purpose and joy.

It is perfectly normal to hurt deep down inside for

that loved one who is trying to live without Christ. Because we know God, we want others to know His love also. But it is possible to agonize too much.

Jesus asked, "Why is my language not clear to you?" Then He answered His own question, "Because you are unable to hear what I say" (John 8:43). If those standing right in front of our Lord Jesus Christ could not hear and understand His words, will everybody hear and understand our words when we talk about Jesus? Our Lord went on to say, "He who belongs to God hears what God says. The reason you do not hear is that you do not belong to God" (8:47). Well, we know that the ungodly don't hear, but they *could*. That's a door that our Lord leaves open. "He who has ears to hear, let him hear," Jesus said.

So on the one hand we ache, we pray for, we long for others, particularly our children. We want them to hear with those spiritual ears. Yet our heads tell us that for some people the other word from Jesus is true as well, "You cannot hear My word." They cannot because they have punctured their own eardrums; they have blocked their own hearing. No matter how clear we make the message, we can tell that they don't get it. It's just as though they cannot hear. This is a tough word from Jesus, a painful message. If refusal to acknowledge God hurts us, think how much more it must hurt our Lord.

Take Down the Walls

We cannot allow walls to be erected between us and our children. Even if walls were once there during their adolescence, those walls have to come down.

One evening in Berlin during the Cold War, I stood near the wall that separated East and West. I said to a

German friend, "What would happen if I walked over there a short distance?" He replied, "You'd be shot." Then one day, by the miracle of God, that wall came down. And it was a miracle. For although the secular press knows nothing of prayer and didn't report it, Christians had been praying for that very thing to happen. The result: euphoria, excitement, ecstasy.

Well, there's another wall that has come down. Paul refers to it in Ephesians 2:14 where he says, "For he himself is our peace, who has made the two one and has destroyed the barrier, the dividing wall of hostility."

Think of it. The wall separating us from God has been torn down. He broke down the wall and said, "Come on through." Through Jesus Christ, He opened the way.

When the wall came down between East and West Berlin, there was a spontaneous national holiday. When people recognize what God has done in Christ Jesus, tearing down the dividing wall of hostility, there is a spontaneous rejoicing as well. We praise, we worship, we say over and over again, "Thank You, God."

Those walls between us and our children need to come down. Hurts, anger, and recollections erect barriers, and Satan will encourage the maintenance of those barriers and the erection of new ones. I have met bitter parents who live in anger toward their children because they can't give up something that really belongs to the immature. They who could be mature adults act like pouting children. Take down the wall. Start praying about it, then go to work. God will help you.

Boomerang Children

Being friends to our children is different than being parents to them. They may be married with children of their own, a stable, happy, functioning family. They may be single parents, divorced, or widowed. They may be poor and we may be called upon to help them. They may be single children, either because they never married or because they had a marriage that went sour. Some are going to return home and move back in with us.

The number of "boomerang children" is increasing. Sometimes they come home with their own children because they cannot afford to live on the wages from a low-paying job. Sometimes they come home because they are unable to find day care at a reasonable cost. Parents who thought their retirement years were free are now full-time caregivers of their grandchildren.

Sometimes children move back in after being away for several years, having gone to college, or a first job. We assumed that our children would have an experience similar to ours; that is, they would know by the time they were twenty or twenty-two what they wanted to do with their lives. They would know who they were as adults, where they wanted to go, and then pursue that choice.

But this expectation is no longer realistic. Every study of the generations born after 1946 shows a state of flux, a refusal to make choices. This is based partly on the multiple options they have, but mostly on a seeming inability or an unwillingness to commit themselves to a certain direction, philosophy, or even to goals. They are explorers doing in their thirties and forties what young people used to do up until age eighteen or twenty. It is not just a midlife crisis; it's more of an adolescent crisis that doesn't end. That's not a put-down, but reality that every social commentator recognizes. When there are so many options, people can become choice-paralyzed. They cannot choose because they might have a better option later on.

Yesterday and Today Don't Compare

There is another side to this fluid state. It's a desire for relationship and connection, a desire to belong, to find oneself, to have roots, to cocoon with one's own family. We are parents to a generation that is being torn. On the one hand they are skeptical about religion and political leadership, the government as a whole, employers, and faithfulness. Many are unwilling to make a commitment, wanting to hang loose, choosing neither career nor spouse, yet wanting to have something of importance in their own lives, someone to love—a baby, another person.

They have deep personal longings, feelings of need, but that doesn't mean they'll connect with us, with the church, or even with God, let alone a permanent career or permanent marriage.

If you are confused by that, so are they. Even though they say that they don't want someone telling them what to do, yet they do want to know what to do.

They crave experiences, and yet experiences don't satisfy. So they're often out looking for new adventures, whether on vacation, in a bar, or just watching a TV program. They don't want absolutes in morals. Many are convinced that the only absolute is that there are no absolutes. Yet, they are longing for some kind of rules and regulations that stop the killings in the streets, that curb the pollution of the environment, that can control the births of drug-addicted babies. If today's young adults are not committed believers by age eighteen, they may very well become Christians at age forty or even fifty. They need to "find themselves," and when that state of flux moves into the midlife years, the drive to find meaning is heightened even more.

That need to "find out who I am" is beginning to

bother some of them. At first it was seen as an end in itself when, in fact, it really isn't an end at all but part of a process. Today we hear more and more talk, not of their wants and needs but of their responsibilities. Be aware of this if you feel your children did not come to right conclusions about life. Those decisions could still be ahead of them.

Sometimes we become angry when we exclaim, "We gave you all these choices." To us choice is a luxury, but they see choice as a necessity. They don't understand that your life pretty well dictated that you needed to get a job and couldn't go to college, or that you had to go into the military and postpone any decisions beyond that, or that you could go to college but had to pay for it yourself. You may have joined a company because they were recruiting on campus, and you stayed with them because you were loyal to them and they to you. Today such loyalty is practically unknown.

If we recognize where we have come from and what has shaped us, and try to recognize what is shaping our children, we'll better be able to make ourselves available to them without trying to run their lives.

Praying for You Too

Your children may be wiser than you think, more mature than you give them credit for, and closer to God than you realize. In fact, it may be that your children are praying for you, especially that you'll understand them. They may be praying that your faith will be deepened. They may have a closer walk with Christ than you have and you don't recognize that walk because it is deeper than your own.

Maybe you have a strong denominational relationship

but not such a deep biblical relationship with Christ. Your children, on the other hand, may have a stronger relationship with Christ than they have to a denomination. None of you are finished with your spiritual growth, and your children may be of help to you.

Recently I read of a woman who had prayed for her father's salvation for years. He was lying ill in the hospital and she was still trying to bring him to faith in Christ. Still he said no. One day the hospital chaplain had a visit with her dad. The next day her father died. The chaplain said, "I've never met anyone so eager to accept Christ."

Just hours before he died, her father had received the Savior. She had longed for his salvation all those years and yet she never did hear his profession of faith. Her father never had the joy of a life lived for Christ, never had the benefits of growing older in the joy of the Lord, but he came to faith. "The Lord is not slow in keeping his promise, as some understand slowness. He is patient with you, not wanting anyone to perish, but everyone to come to repentance" (2 Peter 3:9). Your children may be clinging to this promise in Scripture as they pray for you. They may be asking God, "Why is it taking so long?"

God is patient; He does not quit. God is working in your life and in your children's lives. Parents are always aware of their children, and children, to one degree or another, are always aware of their parents. You say, "Not so. My children have disowned me. They never come around. They don't think of me. They don't write. They don't call. They don't care." That may not be true. They may be needing their space. For whatever reason, they may have needed to get away. They may be terribly involved with their own crises, problems they feel cannot be worked out if a parent is hanging over them. But that doesn't mean they don't care. And it doesn't mean that they don't know you love them.

Prodigals do come home. Miracles, small and large, are occurring every day. Some prodigals have returned late, but they have returned. We need to be alert to the unexpected, to what God may be doing with our children at a moment when we least expect it.

One afternoon in London, Billy Graham telephoned me. He said, "Let's go for a walk." So we walked to Primrose Hill near Regent Park. We talked about children. This man who has been counselor to kings and presidents, and has preached to millions, was interested in my children. He wanted to know how they were growing, maturing, and getting along. As we walked and talked, he spoke of loving our children and added, "Don't ever give up on them."

That conversation took place years ago when my children were still living at home, but I never forgot it. I've repeated those words to myself and used them in conversations with others. To the parents of a fifteen-year-old, I've said, "Don't ever give up on your children." To a parent of a thirty-year-old, I've said, "Don't ever give up on your children." And to a parent of a forty-five-year-old I've said, "Don't ever give up on your children."

Never Meaningless

We cannot be demanding with our grown children. As one older woman said to me one time, "You learn to send advice by slow freight." We learn also that no matter what their age or ours, we are still the only parents our children will ever have. They have longings and expectations of us, just as we have of them. A father one time asked if I would help him influence his daughter by writing to her. He felt that he was an inadequate father and needed others to advise his daughter. I told him that his daughter didn't need advice from strangers. She needed him. He could be her teacher, her guide, her listener. He could love and cherish her.

Where did we get the idea that what we do isn't going to be worth much? I meet older Christians who say, particularly when discussing their children, "My life has been in vain. I have failed. I have not accomplished anything." Well, the Apostle Paul helps us there. In 1 Corinthians 15:58 he states, "Your labor in the Lord is not in vain."

If we have worked to the best of our ability in faithfulness to the Lord, it doesn't matter what we think of the accomplishment. God will honor our work. The world has its own measure of success, but it is not the same as God's measure. We don't decide whether we have been successful in the Lord based on the world's standards. Our labor is not in vain in the Lord if what we do is done for Him. It will never be empty or meaningless or worthless, not even in raising a child.

The question I have to ask myself is, "Am I willing to rise above a situation with my children and see the bigger picture and recognize that God does know the beginning from the end? Will I trust Him and watch what He will do?" What happens to us at any given moment, even if it seems to have been meant for evil, is not the last moment. As believers, we always see ourselves in God's time frame. There is comfort in that thought, especially in tough times.

Just Like Us

One of the realities we have to face is that our children may be more like us than we want to believe. They may think, act, and behave much as we do. We want to help them, but we may want to help them on *our* terms, rarely understanding their terms. But has it occurred to us that they may also want to help us, but on *their* terms? They think they know what is best for us, and they want to protect us, prevent us from doing something harmful, help us with decisions, finances, and all the time we're thinking we need to be helping them. If it is difficult to be a parent of an adult child, it is equally difficult to be an adult child.

One of our greatest acts of love for our children is to let them help us. And one of the best ways to let them do this is to help them see what we really need from them. Not what we demand, but what we really need, so that their love can be expressed to us just as we want to express ours to them. We aren't ever going to be perfect at this job of parenting, but surely we have learned a few things. Age does teach us something.

Age Gives Perspective

Age gives perspective to this business of being a parent. David was old when he wrote "I was young and now I am old" (Psalm 37:25). And in all those years, "I have never seen the righteous forsaken." His psalm contains a key to help us as parents, even in our latter years, "If the Lord delights in a man's way, he makes his steps firm" (v. 23).

God knows exactly where you are, even now. He knows where you have come from with your children, and where you are going. Even more than knowing, David says, "He delights in your way." God not only knows where you are, but He is pleased about where you are. And you can be too.

Because God delights in where you are, verse 24 becomes very personal, "Though he stumble, he will not fall, for the Lord upholds him with his hand." You may trip and fall. As a parent you may make some terrible mistakes, but you won't go crashing down permanently because God is holding your hand. You can get up and try again.

We all trip sometimes, and our first reaction may be, "Why did God let that happen?" But then comes that second thought, "I'm sure glad that God is holding my hand."

In spite of all the changes and confusion of life, God does not change. He is not confused. Underneath all the litter and clutter and debris of life, God is still steady and faithful. With the assurance that God is always caring, always loving, we keep on in our progress as parents. God has not given up on us. We don't give up on ourselves, and we trust that our children won't either.

God loves us and our children. God is patient with us and with our children. Together with each other and with God, we sift through the debris of our lives. God has worked with us all these years; that's how we know that He will continue to help us to be a friend to our children.

Ernie Dempster of Burlington, Ontario is a friend to his children. Your family may be a lot like his.

"I'm seventy-six years old. I've had some physical problems, and last year I lost my wife after fifty-three years of marriage.

"With nine children and twenty-three grandchildren, we've had a remarkable experience in the way God has used them. Our children have testimonies of their own. They minister to perhaps 1,500 people a week.

"My wife and I were always eager to serve. We followed the scriptural injunction to 'use hospitality.' I've continued that and have had fifteen to one hundred people a month in my home in the past year.

"Our kids got a tremendous benefit from the national Christians we invited to our home. I could hear one man praying aloud in his room three hours every night. Things like that rubbed off on the family.

"One of our boys told me that an unsaved man came to him and said, 'Your old man plays his life by the Book.' My son said, 'Dad, that day I made up my mind that my life is going to be like that.'

"A grandson told me, 'The heritage I have from my grandparents is something I can't bypass.'

"I'm gratified."

For Reflection:

1. What walls and barriers between you and your children need to come down? What will be your first step in tearing down those walls?

2. Count some of the ways you see your spiritual influence at work in the lives of your children. Remind yourself to think of that and give thanks the next time you are troubled.

3. How aware are you of your children's needs? Are you praying daily for them?

4. Your children may be praying for you. What do you think they are saying to God?

5. If you do not have children of your own, who are your spiritual adoptees? How are you helping them?

At Last I'm a Grandfather

7

"I love these little people; and it is not a slight thing, when they, who are so fresh from God, love us."
Charles Dickens

"Children have more need of models than of critics."
French proverb

It's 8:45 Thursday morning, and the "grandpas" are arriving at Minnetonka Baptist Church in Minnesota. These volunteers are retired men who have a special ministry to babies and their moms.

As he walks the church hallway pushing a baby stroller, Harold Krantz, who retired after selling his insurance business, says, "It's a mission project. It helps young mothers to get away. I never thought of it as that in the beginning; I thought of it more as baby-sitting. I didn't realize its importance. But there are a lot of mothers who need this time away to visit with other mothers. When I retired, I thought of ministries within my capabilities, finding a niche within the church where I could be effective. I found this niche. I can be a part of this and know I am accomplishing something. I want to be effective, and I feel increasingly that this is my ministry—a ministry of love. I see the joy in the mothers' faces."

This is the day for MOPS, Mothers of PreSchoolers, an outreach to women in the community. "We offer a practical program with Christian examples," a director explains. "We are able to show Christian love and Christian values. For two hours the mothers have a time of teaching, projects to work on, opportunities for discussions with other mothers, and then the Gospel is presented. They hear the Good News."

That's possible because the "grandpas" and many women, some of whom are grandmothers, take care of the nursery, the toddlers, and the preschoolers, allowing the moms the freedom to hear the Good News.

Louis Freeman, another grandpa, says, "It's a ministry that a guy can do. I do Meals on Wheels and drive the shuttle bus for the Senior Citizens Center. I do lawns for people who are unable to do their own and call on people in the hospital. It's amazing when you check around how much you can do for people. A Christian ought to have a continuing ministry. When I retired, I looked for volunteer jobs, and this is a ministry I can do. Don't call on me to do carpenter work, but I can rock a baby."

One of the grandmothers volunteering with the little ones is Jean Betz. She explains, "We used to have neighborhoods where we could get together as mothers and talk. Now moms don't have other moms around to talk with, but they can come here. I believe this program is a wonderful outreach."

And so while grandmas are in the nursery, the grandpas walk back and forth out in the halls pushing strollers or carrying a crying child until he or she settles down. "It's something we can do," they say. "It's our ministry."

We are all grandpas or grandmas, whether we have grandchildren of our own or not, because there are so many babies and children who need us.

There may be children living in our neighborhoods whose parents both work, or children of single parents who are trying to make ends meet. These children are out on the streets or they have a key on a string around their necks to let themselves in after school. Could they come to your house? Some older people say, "I don't have a ministry because I'm not able to get out." But this could be a ministry where you don't have to go out. Children can come to you if you establish a relationship with them and their parents first. Instead of children being home alone, they can do their homework at your dining room table. You can serve them cookies and milk after school. You can sing with them, listen to them, hear their hurts from the day. You have a need for a bigger world and they have a need for your care and love.

If there are children on your street who do not have a place to go after school, will you someday wonder, "How did they turn into such delinquents? Why do they commit crimes?" Maybe you could have been the believing Christian to bring them into your home after school. You still can, no matter what your age. There are stories they'd love to hear. You have a different voice than Mom or Dad; you could give the kind of understanding counsel that they might hear.

The Value of a "Dirty Barn"

I asked some grandparents, "Why aren't more people caring for neighborhood children?" They replied, "Our friends tell us, 'We didn't retire to work. We took care of our children. It's enough for us when our own grandchildren visit. We're tired.' " But then they admit that these older people are usually the same ones who have no physical, emotional, or spiritual outlet, who usually become bitter and introspective, who develop health problems that consume more and more of their emotional energy.

"No, I won't open my house," an older person says. "Children are a nuisance. Children are dirty. Children clutter. Children disrupt my routine."

Solomon made an interesting comment on life, "Where there are no oxen, the manger is empty, but from the strength of an ox comes an abundant harvest" (Proverbs 14:4). You can have a clean barn if you don't have any animals in it, but you won't have a profitable farm. And you can have a neat, clean, uncluttered life if there are no people (especially children) in your life. But will you also lack a ministry?

Get with people and you will get with their problems, but that's also when you will have a successful, productive ministry. Eliminate people from your life, focus only on yourself and, like the farmer with no oxen, your surroundings might be neat and clean but you won't produce anything. So the next time you complain about all the people and their children who keep invading your life, think about the farmer who complains that he has a dirty barn. Do you really want an uncluttered life? Do you really want to have no ministry? Give thanks to God for the people and their children who "clutter up" your life.

A Contribution We Can Make

Why did God allow us to have the wisdom, the time, the spiritual experience, and the biblical knowledge He gave us, if not for others? Since there is little opportunity for religious teaching in the schools and, in fact, a lot of teaching that is antireligious, wouldn't it be wonderful if a child coming home from school could talk about what he heard with a "grandma" or "grandpa" next door or down the street, instead of going home to an empty house and a television set? Wouldn't it be wonderful if that child could have the Scriptures opened to her and could hear about the living Lord Jesus Christ?

Child Evangelism Fellowship knows full well that a child can understand the Gospel at a very early age. They have built a ministry on it. Many Christian leaders have said that they were converted as little children or brought to faith through the witness of their own young children. Evangelical leader John Perkins is an example of a man who came to faith through the witness of his young son who was led to Christ by children's workers.

We can help youngsters become better integrated into a truly biblical understanding of life; we can give them some parameters for their lives, ideas that they can test, other ways of thinking than they are getting on the streets, and a safe haven when there may be pain for them at home. But to be that "safe haven," a retired person has to want to be available and to understand that "God didn't put me here just to take up space and think only of myself." He or she has to know, "God has placed me here for ministry, and this is where I must serve."

Some say, "I can't and I won't because I'm hurting so much myself. My children have hurt me; my own adult children are still in rebellion. They won't grow up." But is that an excuse not to keep opening your arms and the door of your home to others? Work with the children God gives you today. Even if you have had a bad experience—a child stealing from you or cursing you—don't assume another child will be that way too.

A Wonderful Army for Good

If we want to be missionaries we have to understand the culture we go into, and if we are going to be grandparents, we have to understand those younger than we are and recognize they are a different culture too. We may have a lot of learning to do; but as missionaries to children, we have reason not to let our growing stop.

Praise God that many are saying "yes" to the opportunities around them to be grandmas and grandpas. They don't act old, just mature. They recognize that the over-sixty-five population, which in the United States is now moving toward fifty million, is a wonderful army for good. That means no child should be without a grandparent on his street or in his church or at the teen drop-in center. No young parent should be without an older encourager or helper nearby.

There are more and more volunteer grandparenting opportunities available. In fact, as social welfare funds become less available, the need for such volunteers increases. Christians who know this realize that they are a tremendous resource for influence and wisdom, and so they give themselves to their community, especially to the children.

A study published in *Psychology Today* talks about the need for people to have a sacred dimension to their lives. It talks about memories and about fitting the sacred into life, not allowing religion to be removed.[1] They call it "vernacular spirituality," the need to bring in traditions and beliefs and teachings because they give balance so that there is less psychological adjustment later on. We who have the years and who are alive in Christ have that needed balance that people want, even crave. We can offer it.

Children—Just Like Us

Jesus loved the little children. Matthew 18 shows us that Jesus drew a little child to Him and said, "I tell you the truth, unless you change and become like little children, you will never enter the kingdom of heaven" (v. 3).

As I have watched our grandchildren, I know that the example Jesus used is absolutely perfect. Our grandchildren are trusting, dependent, loving, and eager to learn. That makes me look at myself as a child of God and ask, "Am I trusting, am I dependent and loving, am I eager to learn?"

Jesus never said to become childish; He told us to become "like little children." There is a difference. Watch a little child. That is what Jesus wants of you and me.

Our Children's Children

Studies show that today 70 percent of people over sixty-five are grandparents. For some that means children living away at a distance; for others grandchildren are within easy visiting distance. For still others, the grandchildren are living in the grandparents' home, and that number is increasing. More than two million grandparents have grandchildren living in their homes. It may not be what they planned for their retirement years, but the children are there and they need love.

A Christian psychologist, reflecting on grandparents who unexpectedly find themselves "parents" again, said that most are not angry about it but accept it as an opportunity. "They are committed to raising the children with love," he said. "Instead of seeing the grandchildren as an unexpected intrusion—just at the time when they thought they could relax and have a life of their own, there are children around again—grandparents see the young ones as a ministry." He added, "I don't find them angry at God or resentful."

That there are problems associated with grandchildren moving in with grandparents is clear. Sometimes the grandparents don't know the father of their grandchildren, or one of the parents is in trouble with the law. Sometimes the problems are economic or involve severe illness or death. Yet grandparents do seem to be willing to take care of youngsters again. They understand that God knows what is happening and His words are proven true, "My grace is sufficient for you" (2 Corinthians 12:9).

Grandparents with grandchildren at home are known as second-time-around parents, which is also the name of some support groups being formed around the country for caregivers who are grandparents. They are the ones who have to handle the responsibilities of bringing their grandchildren to school, and may have all the responsibilities for child-care—legally, financially, and emotionally—along with the fatigue from not being as young as they once were. It can happen early; parents in their forties and fifties become primary caregivers because their child had a baby she or he could not take care of. They may even be AIDS babies or crack babies. Or they may be junior high kids whose parents are in prison. It can happen late, with teens moving in with grandparents because their parents are having marital problems. A University of California-Berkeley professor said there could be as many as four million children in the United States in the care of grandparents, an increase of 40 percent over the last ten years. The AARP has several national grandparent groups, offering help and support for grandparents who are primary care-givers for their grandchildren.

A Crown to the Aged

As our children get older and have children of their own, most of them begin to appreciate their parents. So we grandparents have two wonderful experiences—we have the crowning joy of grandchildren and the increasing appreciation of our own children. They have moved past their own youth and have begun to understand something of life and a few things about their parents. One grandmother said, "My son told me recently, 'I don't know how you did it.'"

I'm old enough now to recognize the truth in a verse of Scripture that I never understood when I was young. In Proverbs 17:6 I read, "Children's children are a crown to the aged, and parents are the pride of their children." Now that I am a grandfather, I understand that "children's children are a crown."

We love our grandchildren and boast about them. We have much to offer them. We have ourselves and that's the best offering. We can be supportive, we can listen, we can offer counsel, all the time recognizing that the little ones belong to our children, not to us. Still, we have what a harried parent doesn't have—the gift of time—for our children and our grandchildren.

A Teaching Privilege

But whether a child is living in our home, just around the corner, or miles away, we have a teaching privilege that is special. Studies show that the grandparent-grand-child bond is one of the strongest emotional attachments. What a valuable opportunity that gives grandparents—a second chance.

There are many opportunities to teach. If your grandchild is miles away, write letters. Letters and notes are so special to children because they realize it is something sent "to me alone, with my name on it." That letter or note will be cherished, read again and again. Put your love in it, tell about yourself, explain your own beliefs—and ask about them.

Children love telephone calls. They can tell about their day—a happy event or a sad one, an accomplishment, a victory or a failure. When Grandpa or Grandma calls, just for them, that's special.

Grandchildren want to learn about us. "What was it like when you were a little boy, Grandpa?" they want to know.

Tell them about yourself. Tell them why you believe as you do. When you're together, show them pictures, books, objects that you had when you were younger, and tell them why those items are important. Prepare a family autobiography for them. It will give them a sense of heritage. And adding your own testimony to your heritage may be the first Gospel presentation they have.

If you can, bring your grandchildren to your home for a week or two. This gives their parents a break and gives you some quality time. You and your grandchildren can go to the zoo together, watch a video, go to Sunday School, play games, go fishing, talk about what's really important. The child will never forget those times. If you doubt it, think about the times that you visited your grandparents.

That Wonderful Gift

Having grandchildren around can be wonderful or stressful. It can be a time of loving or a time of hurting.

In the Book of Ruth, Naomi was given a word about her grandson that changed her whole outlook on life. "He will renew your life and sustain you in your old age" (Ruth 4:15). Well, that happened. Naomi had lots of problems. She was a widow. She lost both her sons. But when Ruth married Boaz, Naomi was given a grandson who brought new meaning to her life.

There are never surprises with God, and if He has given you grandchildren, then He will also give you the strength and wisdom to be a good grandparent, and the ability to handle situations, even if you have to be the primary caregiver. And God will give you the blessing when your grandchild "renews your life."

There is something wonderful about our children's children. As grandparents, we not only learn something new about our children when they become parents, but we learn a lot about ourselves from our grandchildren. They renew us and bring us joy. Isn't that a wonderful gift that God gives in the latter years of our lives? One of the nicest things the psalmist could wish for was, "May you live to see your children's children" (Psalm 128:6).

Our grandchildren need to hear the Gospel. They need to hear it even when they are little and we tell it to them in story form. They need biblical heroes. They need to hear about missionaries and Christians who have made a difference in business or industry or medicine or the arts. We can tell them.

Grandchildren need to have someone with time enough to hear them talk out or act out in play what they are thinking and wondering about. Even if we didn't have that time when we were busy parents, we can provide it now to our grandchildren.

If we're not the primary caregivers of our own grandchildren but we know people who are caring for theirs, we can offer a needed and effective ministry by supporting their grandparenting, giving them a change, a chance to get away. We can offer our care and love to their grandchildren by "adopting" them as a larger family.

We have much to give our own grandchildren and the grandchildren of others. They'll look forward to trips we make to their house. They'll look forward to money gifts, to our attendance at special events such as graduation. With their parents' approval, we can give the gift of a week at a Christian camp or a weekend retreat. They'll look forward to phone calls on birthdays or a call when you can say, "Congratulations" for an athletic achievement or scholastic award.

We can offer memory gifts—an old baseball glove that Grandpa had as a boy, a fountain pen that Grandmother used years ago. We can encourage them by asking for drawings and letters from them, or handmade crafts. We can display what they give us.

Do all grandchildren know the heartbeat of their grandparents? Some don't know that their grandparents care, because they never see examples of it. Some grandparents have turned responsibility around and have said selfishly, "They don't remember me. They don't talk to me. They don't call me. They don't pay attention to me." But who's the adult? Who should take the initiative?

When there's divorce, a split family, single parents, or blended families, don't take sides or divide children and parents. Be supportive of parents' struggles and their tough economic times, especially if both parents have to

work. Offer advice only when asked. Don't turn everything around to your own pain and troubles. If they talk
about an illness, don't use it as a launch to talk about
your own illness. Get into their world; don't keep demanding that they get into yours.

Skipping to the Next Generation

Recently I met some teenagers who were talking about
television. One said, "Oh, we rarely watch television. It
isn't real." I thought, *The generation ahead of you seems to
think that television is very real.* Obviously the young ones
are not following the older. Maybe we need to look at
each generation with new eyes and recognize that just
as in the kingdom of Judah God brought a change with
the next generation, He may be doing the same today.

In reading the Old Testament, I have noticed that
goodness and faithfulness often skip a generation. One
person serves the Lord; his children do not, but his
grandchildren do. That came back to me again as I was
reading 2 Chronicles 34:1-2, "Josiah was eight years old
when he became king, and he reigned in Jerusalem thir-
ty-one years." Although his own father was terribly
wicked, Josiah "did what was right in the eyes of the
Lord and walked in the ways of his father David, not
turning aside to the right or to the left." We care about
our children, but some may be like King Amon. We need
to care about our grandchildren too; they may be future
Josiahs. They are an investment we must not miss.

Ecclesiastes 3 tells us, "There is a time for everything,
and a season for every activity under heaven . . . a time
to weep and a time to laugh, a time to mourn and a time
to dance" (vv. 1, 4).

This is God's time for us—a grandparenting time.

Now we have to ask, "Are we in this grandparenting time of life with God?" If we are, it will be a wonderful time.

For Reflection:

1. To whom are you a grandparent? Did you name only your biological grandchildren? Should there be others too?

2. Do you know struggling grandparents who are having to be second-time-around parents? How can you help them?

3. What memories are you building in the lives of children—on your street, in your church, in your family?

4. Are you consciously offering a spiritual inheritance to the grandchildren God has given you? How are you teaching them?

5. How's your focus? Do you think of grandchildren as "there to help me"? Or are you concentrating on ways to help them?

Together Is Good; Alone Is Good Too

8

"Marriage is not a state, but a movement —
a boundless adventure."
Paul Tournier

"People who cannot bear to be alone are the worst company."
Albert Guinon

Winter is coming, and Bill and Arlene Hatch are preparing their recreational vehicle to travel south. Their trip isn't just for sun and fun—they are also going to work. They join a band of retirees who, throughout the winter, move from ministry to ministry, serving two or three weeks in each place, helping in a missionary office with mailings, volunteering their enthusiasm and their skills to the Christian agencies that need their help. These agencies are so eager for them that they provide camper hookups for people with RVs. No camper? That's OK. A lot of places provide condominium housing for those who will come and work.

One couple who work with migrants, food pantries, and other projects, commented, "We believe in James 1:22, being doers of the Word and not hearers only. It's our philosophy that people ought to be out working. We have an abundance of pew sitters."

Dr. Hugh Westgate and his wife, Alison, work together on ministry projects that take them to countries where they not only serve but leave something lasting behind. Alison says, "In 1981 we went on a fact-finding trip to five countries in Africa. We had some great experiences, but Hugh realized that he is not a village medical person; it wasn't his gift. He teaches anesthesiology at the universities wherever he goes and also does some medical work. By teaching, we leave something behind when we leave. We planned to do this kind of ministry our entire life, and we prepared for it financially.

"In 1983 Hugh went with the Minnesota International Health Volunteers to Uganda and came back a changed man. We vowed that we would go together from then on, even though I do not have a medical background. The first time I didn't fit in. I said, 'Here I am, God; what will I do?' I ended up teaching English as a second language. A year later I thought I was to teach, but when I arrived, school was not in session. So I spent my time as a counselor, which is what I do for a living.

"God uses your talents—wherever you are. I volunteer at home too, not just overseas. I was a volunteer probation officer for fifteen years. Now I'm a custody mediator.

"We believe in doing something at home as well as overseas. There is so much to be done in our own city too. I have volunteered from four to forty hours a week. There are 3,000 volunteer opportunities in our own Hennepin County alone. There isn't a talent in the world that God can't use somewhere. We believe in being in the marketplace where the people are. We're going to do international work as long as we are useful."

Hugh says, "I believe I have a responsibility to pass on to others the good that has been given to me. I have a responsibility to teach. I have a responsibility to worship God with everything that I have and to serve my fellow-man as Christ has taught.

"I want to pass on God's Word. I have a unique opportunity because as a medical teaching guest in another country I can talk about my belief in Christ and His relationship to me.

"To live effectively you have to keep advancing toward something. To quit is a death knell. The person who does that is running away from something. If you retire to escape problems, you don't survive very long. Your responsibility is to share knowledge and help others. When you do that, you will grow and your retirement years will be pleasant."

Dull or Exciting—Which Will It Be?

You have been married for years; you know each other well. For some that becomes dull, boring, a relationship to be taken for granted. After a few months of golf and travel, you sit at home and become an annoyance to each other.

But there are works to be accomplished. There are people to help, ministries where you can serve—and God has given you a unique contribution to make. As husband and wife, you are not alike—that's what attracted you to each other in the first place. And through the years God has developed your gifts, your talents, to be used in special ways.

There are things a husband does that a wife doesn't do. There are things she does that he doesn't do. He may be more business-oriented, she more people-centered. He may be more into construction; she may be better gifted in teaching or in crafts, but they are a ministry team. They work together at home, helping each other, contributing to the work around the house, giving time for each to be able to study, grow, and be engaged in ministry.

Some people fear that retirement will mean getting on one another's nerves. But we can have the best that marriage offers in our senior years when we no longer have the duties of child-rearing, when the workplace no longer calls, when we have liberty to give our gifts to others, when together we can put to use all that we have learned through our lifetime. Many couples find a new depth to their companionship and a new appreciation for the partner's gifts.

In the "Neighbors" section of *The Wichita Eagle*, November 18, 1993, was a story about Bernice and Don Mead who work together as volunteers for the Red Cross. Their service has taken them to nine disaster sites in fifteen months. In the interview with reporter Roz Hutchinson, Don Mead said, "Common sense and life skills really come in handy. And knowing how to make people who never had to ask for anything feel at ease." Bernice says she's simply "being a good neighbor. I ask them, 'You'd help me if I lived next door, wouldn't you? Well, I've just come a little farther, that's all.' People ask, 'Why do you go?' and I say, 'Because I'm selfish. I get so much out of it.' "[1]

Valma Volz discovered that she and her husband could exercise their different gifts and still encourage one another when she retired before her husband did. "I took early retirement saying, 'Okay, Lord, use me wherever You see fit.' His hand has been with me all the way. It has been incredible.

"My career meant a lot to me, but there came a time in my life when I said, 'Well, I've enjoyed this; I've done the things I've wanted to do, but there is something more to life.'

"I'm doing training for the Salvation Army, and that involves a lot of weekend travel. My husband and I discussed it at length and he is really supportive. He says, 'Wherever you feel the Lord is leading, I'm with you.'

"As long as I'm healthy and can manage, I will keep doing this. I'd say to people who retire and are not doing ministry, 'Think again; you don't know what you're missing.' I have a deep conviction that our calling is a lifetime calling. I don't see a time limit on whatever gifts we have to offer to the Lord, as long as we can manage physically and mentally.

"Each of us is gifted in some way. It's a disservice and certainly poor stewardship not to use those gifts even into retirement. Some wise people once said to me, 'Think back to yourself as a teenager or young adult. Who made the greatest impact on your life? It was always someone who was mature.' So I think maybe I can make a difference in a small way. I know I can, with the Lord's help."

There is a passage of Scripture that offends some people, but it shouldn't. It is Proverbs 18:22, which reads, "He who finds a wife finds what is good [some versions read "good thing"] and receives favor from the Lord." What bothers people is that "a wife isn't some thing that's 'found.' " And that's true enough. But we speak of finding success or finding happiness and treasure and blessing, and these are all parts of what a man gains when he finds a wife. So the word "find" isn't so bad. If I was looking for treasure and found it, it wouldn't negate the value of the treasure by saying I found it.

Others are offended by a wife being a good "thing." Well, she's not the "thing" referred to. She is a good thing for her husband. What the husband finds is a good thing *for* him; she is a blessing from the Lord. I have found that to be true in my life and I know a lot of other men have also. "He who finds a wife finds what is good and receives favor from the Lord." That might be old-fashioned wording, but the idea is timeless.

Husbands and wives enhance each other, build each other, complement and contribute to each other. Retirement is a good time to build on the marriage foundation with new shared experiences. Those experiences need to include investment in other people's lives and in Christian ministry.

An Example That Others See

A couple can each have their own ministry. In 1972, Howard Bentall, Senior Minister of First Baptist Church, Calgary, Alberta, retired. But for the next twenty years he volunteered his services to the Baptist Union of Western Canada. Then he and his wife, Shirley, moved to Vancouver where he is now on the staff of Carey Theological College.

"I just turned eighty," he says. "My health is 100 percent. I'll just carry on as long as I can. I love it. People would live longer if they carried on. I'm sure my health is partly attributable to the fact that I didn't stop.

"Shirley has her own career as a conference speaker and writer. She was president of the Baptist Union, president of the Canadian Baptist Federation, and currently she is Canadian Vice-President of the Baptist World Alliance. She is also writing her fifth book. She has her own portfolio, which is almost a full-time one. Our involvement in our local church is together. It has been a fulfilling and enjoyable retirement. I don't want to stop; I just want to carry on until I drop."

Husbands and wives need to allow each other opportunities to exercise their gifts individually and separately, not clinging to each other, not insisting that where one goes the other must go also.

In an article in *Christianity Today*, a comment was made that couples who have been married for thirty, forty, fifty years have a great resource that others need to draw upon. The writer tells about sex education being taught in the school classroom. Children say they'd really like to meet people who have been married a long time and who have kept their love alive. They want to see living examples. The author suggests that we who have had a long and happy marriage go into high schools or junior highs and let the students ask us what makes our marriage strong and why it has lasted.[2] What a wonderful opportunity to talk about the foundation of our marriage, which is Jesus Christ. We can tell them how serving God and worshiping together is part of growing together. In a time when a rain forest or a bird is seen as endangered and needing to be protected, many do not see marriage in the same way. Long-term marriages teach not only about falling in love but also growing in love.

If our marriages can be an example in the schools and our work together can be a service to ministries, what we illustrate as a married couple, individually or separately, can make a difference to others in our community. So can our worship. For people are watching that too.

The Prophet Micah explains what we do when we worship, and why we do it. "Come, let us go up to the mountain of the Lord, to the house of the God of Jacob. He will teach us his ways, so that we may walk in his paths" (4:2).

God wants us to come to His mountain, to His house of worship. He wants to teach us His ways. He wants to show us, encourage us, bless us. He wants us to walk in His ways. He wants more than that, of course, for walking in His ways means enjoying Him, worshiping Him, serving Him, obeying Him. That is a meaningful part of our time in the house of God—the worship, the adoration, the praise, the renewal of the commitment that says, "I will walk in Your paths." That's good for us as individuals as well as for our marriage. That's good for others who know us and for those who watch us from a distance.

Memories

My wife and I share memories from our past even as we build memories right now through ministering to others together. Recently Andrea and I went back to the city where she spent her childhood. It was like a walk down Memory Lane, as we went to the places where she lived as a girl, to the school she attended. We even went to the playground where she and her sister played.

It was wonderful to go back, but there was another side to the remembering, for she wasn't a believer then. She became a Christian after moving from that city. It is good to remember where we were, where we came from, and where we are now. Hebrews 10:32 says, "Remember those earlier days after you had received the light, when you stood your ground in a great contest in the face of suffering." That's part of our memory too—recalling what it was like to come to faith in Christ—to be a believer in a setting of unbelievers. That was my wife's experience. It was mine too.

Memories help us to know where we have been in our spiritual journey. They help us to rejoice in all that we have today in Christ. That's what Andrea and I learned on that trip down Memory Lane.

But we are building memories too. When we travel together to a ministry work, we not only experience it and rejoice in it, but we can then talk about it afterward, because it was shared. And that makes a difference in our praying.

Ready for Life Alone?

For some people, though, the memories of a marriage are all they have left. People who have been married for many years find themselves feeling lost when their partner dies. My own dad died at age sixty-seven; my mother, even twenty years later, is still speaking of "when Dad was alive."

It takes a long time for grief to go away. When one loses a loved one, the loss is always there; pain surfaces any time of day, no matter what else is happening. In their grieving some people are angry at God. But those who know God well know that He is there loving them. He is present. "When my prayers returned to me unanswered, I went about mourning. . . . I bowed my head in grief," said the psalmist (Psalm 35:13-14). Maybe so, but not forever. Mourning doesn't last forever.

Are you ready for life alone? Have you prepared for it? Have you talked to each other about how you will deal with the death of your partner?

My dad died suddenly, with no warning, no time to prepare. Others have long, lingering illnesses with opportunity to talk about death and prepare for it. If the remaining spouse is strong and has a ministry, that can continue. We don't have to quit when we lose our partner. We recognize that God knows exactly where we are, that He doesn't change; although we're now without a partner, the abilities God gave to us are still there. The calling is too. The promise given to Joshua is the promise given to us, "As I was with Moses, so I will be with you; I will never leave you nor forsake you" (Joshua 1:5). He will never leave us. Even if we are widowed, we still have a life to live for Christ until we too are taken home.

Holda Fast of Clearbrook, British Columbia knows that. She's a widow now, but she continues to be a blessing to her denomination, to her church, and to individuals who need what she has to offer. "When my husband died in 1989, the church where I served as minister of music gave me a one-year sabbatical to be more private and allow myself to heal. I found that was a good thing for me to do. Then I went back with renewed energy.

"Now I do a lot of workshops on worship. I'm also part of the editing committee for the new denominational hymnal which is going into production. I see myself as a facilitator, to give counsel and advice and to be available to churches.

"I think grief accentuates if you allow yourself to hold to home and house. I don't think that honors the person you have loved for years. I've tried to do what would honor my husband. I'm a very optimistic person; I grieved, but there is also a lot of joy.

"It is good for our children to see that their mom continues to have energy and vigor and a sense of ministry, that she is not going to lie down and die.

"I don't believe in putting people on the shelf. We have a different input at different stages in life. And I think I have more to offer now than I did twenty years ago because of my experience and what I have gone through. People tell me I have something to offer and I want to continue giving."

Limitations Don't Have to Stop Us

I know an elderly pastor who is widowed now. But even while his wife was alive, he was mostly alone. He could not travel or open his home to others. His wife was ill and needed care for many years, and he lived in a retirement center where his wife was cared for in the nursing wing. He spent his afternoons with her and they ate their evening meal together.

But he could go out and teach a Sunday School class. He could do interim preaching in nearby churches. He could do home visitation and make hospital calls for one of the churches. His limits were real, but so were his opportunities.

Few have the absolute freedom to do everything they might wish to do. But each can say, "Lord, here I am." For whatever door God opens, His requirement of us is that we be available, faithful, and willing servants.

We have to be ready for life alone. That's why it's good while we're together to help our spouse develop his or her ministry. Women may be good at teaching other women while the husband is helping at home or praying. Habitat for Humanity, which has a wonderful ministry of building and repairing houses for people, has used couples or men alone or women alone. In my city, I know of a house that was built entirely by women.

Some men who are good at helping men are able to do it because a wife is willing to spend an evening or two alone or has a ministry of her own. There are women who don't want to travel but won't hold back their husbands who see missionary opportunities abroad. There are men who don't want their wives to travel alone and are glad to accompany them even though they don't feel qualified for the ministry opportunity. When spouses have helped each other develop abilities, then when one spouse is alone, those abilities will continue to be applied to some of the wonderful and fulfilling ministry opportunities God offers.

What about people who have always lived alone? Sometimes it is difficult for a single person to muster sympathy for a husband or wife who loses a spouse after forty-five or fifty years of marriage. "Now they're where I've always been," says the single person.

Whether they've always been alone or are alone for the first time in decades, many have discovered that it is good to be alone. God's promise, "Your Maker is your husband" (Isaiah 54:5), takes on special meaning for them. The words of Jesus, "I will ask the Father, and he will give you another Counselor to be with you forever" (John 14:16), prove especially true. "Never will I leave you; never will I forsake you" (Hebrews 13:5) has a new dimension to it.

One day in my newspaper I saw a story about a seventy-seven-year-old hospital volunteer named Eleanor Whitmyre. She has more than 13,000 hours as a volunteer, answering phones and talking with cancer patients. One hospital supervisor described her as "the closest thing to Jesus Christ I've ever met." This dynamic volunteer says she has always been single, never had children, and learned long ago, "You'd better make your own happiness." So she does, obeying the words of Micah 6:8, which she carries on a card in her purse: "What does the Lord require of you? To act justly and to love mercy, and to walk humbly with your God."

She is alone in her ministry, yet not alone. She says, "My life is very full. I'm not lonely at all."[3]

Think of Others

A person alone can either grow or wither, look out to new horizons and expand, or look inward and become narrow. Recently I watched an elderly widow and a younger widow going out to dinner together and realized the discovery they were making. Each was contributing to the other from the perspective of her own generation, yet they had something in common.

Another widow knew she would never have the ministry that she and her husband once shared together. And she realized that the house they had lived in for so many years was too much for one person alone, especially as she grew weaker with age. So she made her plans and moved to a retirement center where she began a Bible study ministry with other women who were in similar circumstances. They knew she understood their needs; she knew they needed encouragement from God's Word. She proved that the steps of a good person are ordered by the Lord. She could have spent her years complaining, but she spent them serving as a Bible teacher, encouraging and edifying others.

Others are left alone because after years of marriage and the raising of children, one spouse has decided, "I don't want to be married to you anymore." It's particularly hard if the man is the one who has left and the wife, who had committed herself to a lifetime of home-making, has little retirement income and few benefits. She is poor, struggling, and hurting.

It is difficult to say to her, "Think of others." Yet there is a ministry in thinking of others that helps a person with his or her own hurts. Working as a volunteer with children who are dying of cancer, helping to make their last days comfortable, takes a person away from herself and gives a wonderful sense of value. "I'm needed" is a respectable reason for serving.

You may find opportunities in your church, at a mission, or in a ministry that needs clerical help or other skills. It may not bring in income, but it does say loud and clear, "Lord, You have invested in me, and my life is not over. Therefore, I will invest in the lives of others."

Some older people still living in their homes rent space to students. They may be willing to do household chores as partial payment. This also gives an older person security at night and a feeling of peace that "If I become ill, someone is here to call for help." What a ministry it is, at mealtime or in the evening, to be able to talk with a student and to tell why life in Christ is so rich and beautiful and good.

Age Can't Stop a Ministry of Prayer

Some people have a ministry using only the telephone. I knew a woman who lived for years in an iron lung. A voice-activated telephone was her link to the world; particularly, it was her link to a ministry through prayer.

Men have telephoned me to ask, "How may I pray for you?" and then did pray for me, right there on the phone. I have cherished those times. Prayer lists are a vital missionary work. Because prayer knows no boundaries, we can pray for workers in Africa, Asia, or Latin

America, and know that God even then is answering that prayer—empowering, helping, and encouraging that person so many miles away. Talking to others on the phone expands our world. We can be there with them in spirit, reaching out, assisting, praying, and offering help.

And often the next call is to a church prayer group with the words, "I have a friend on the mission field who has a need. Could you bring that need to your prayer group or circle at church?" Many have such a linking ministry in their older years.

Eric Crichton, for twenty-three years pastor of Calvary Church in Lancaster, Pennsylvania, talks about the ministry of prayer and letter writing. He sees the value because he knows missionaries. "I just got back from Japan where I spoke at three Keswick conventions. The month before I was in Monte Carlo filling in at an English-speaking church.

"I'm not doing anything spectacular; I'm just carrying on ministry begun when I was at the church. I don't believe you retire from serving the Lord. So long as the Lord gives me health and strength, I'm happy to keep doing this. The Apostle Paul wanted to finish well; I'd like to finish well too.

"Sitting around doing nothing would be terrible. Retired people have special opportunities and can give a lot more time to prayer. What greater ministry is there for missions today than praying for the world? And people can correspond. One minister I know, a Bible teacher in Scotland, sends seven postcards every day to missionaries. Think what that means to people! I tell older people to get on with it; there is so much to do to serve the Lord in retirement."

He's right. There is.

For Reflection:

1. How are you helping your spouse prepare for a retirement ministry?

2. You know retired couples who get on each other's nerves. How can you start now to avoid that?

3. What ministries have you and your spouse planned for this year? Next year?

4. Have you talked with your spouse about the ministry you would like to have after you are widowed or you are too frail to be active? Are you helping each other to get ready?

Never Stop Growing

9

*"Unless you try to do something beyond what you
have already mastered, you will never grow."*
Ronald E. Osborn

"Why stay we on earth except to grow?"
Robert Browning

Geoff Still, President of Focus on the Family, Canada,
was "retired"—and enjoying every minute of it. Before
his death in January 1995, he said, "I retired at age fifty-
seven in 1982. In June of that year, I went to an event
regarding bringing Billy Graham to Vancouver for a crusade. I agreed to help get the ball rolling and became the
executive chairman of that crusade.

"When the crusade was over, I discovered that I had
prostate cancer. Early in 1985 I had surgery for cancer. I
came out of the hospital on March 12 and that same day
got a call from David Mainse of the Christian telecast
"100 Huntley Street" which originates in Toronto. He

asked me if I would be general manager and deputy commissioner of the Pavilion of Promise at Expo '86 in Vancouver. It gave me such a lift to think that there was something I could do. So, for eighteen months I served in that capacity.

"As that was ending, Dr. James Dobson asked what my plans were after Expo. I replied, 'Perhaps I can help Focus on the Family.'" At sixty-nine, Geoff Still was in his eighth year with Focus on the Family (Canada) Association.

"One of the hardest things for me is to see retirees looking aimlessly in store windows. I see the boredom on their faces. Retirees who aren't doing ministry make me wonder how they can have a sense of meaning in life and fulfillment. Some of my Christian friends who play golf five days a week tell me that they long to be doing what I'm doing. They say to me, 'I don't feel my life has any meaning. I don't feel as though I have anything important to do.'

"I've changed over the years. When I was younger my idea of retirement was to go to the lake all summer, to play golf, and then go to Florida in the winter. I don't think I could do that anymore.

"God has really blessed me. I feel so overwhelmed at what I'm doing. I marvel at the grace of God in allowing me to be involved in these wonderful projects.

"That's where real worth is. If a person wants zest in his life, that's it. My wife, Beverly, appreciates the fact that I am so fulfilled. I think it's good for my health too. Each day holds so many blessings for me and so many thrills.

"So I don't think I'll ever retire. I'll just take one day at a time. In 1982 I never planned on doing anything other than retiring. Everything from then on has been a surprise."

You're Not Useless

Do you think you're too old to have a ministry? You've been on the shelf for a while, long retired, useless? Well, you might be old, but you're not useless.

Nedine Kolmodin, with her retired pastor husband, Ken, have volunteered at a missionary agency and served as call-ins for local ministries near their home. Ken has served as a volunteer chaplain at a nursing home and has done interim pastoral work, most recently in Michigan, where Nedine also serves one day a week at a rescue mission and another day at a nonprofit relief agency. Ask them where ministry opportunities are, and they can bring out mission agency brochures, letters from friends, and denominational requests, to show that retirees have only to say, "Here I am." Nedine says, "I have to have a reason to get up in the morning. There are so many needs."

To the Kolmodins, and thousands of others who are free to stretch and grow and serve, the question is never, "Do I have what it takes?" In Christ each mature believer has what it takes. The only question is what and how much am I willing to do and where I will do it.

Take a look at a biblical "retiree" named Daniel. Belshazzar the king made a great feast. You remember the story . . . when the handwriting came on the wall and nobody could figure it out. Then the queen mother remembered, "There is a man in your kingdom who has the spirit of the holy gods in him. In the time of your father he was found to have insight and intelligence and wisdom like that of the gods" (Daniel 5:11).

Now realize that Daniel hadn't been heard from in about twenty-five years. He was in his eighties, but he was still God's man. He had God's understanding, he had God's wisdom, and he was ready. Look at how the Lord used him. Daniel spoke the truth to the king. It wasn't a happy truth but it was a necessary one.

You may be in your eighties. You may not have been heard from in years. Are you faithful? Can God call on you as He needs you? Are you ready? Daniel was. God knows His faithful ones, no matter how old they are.

Useless? Unfruitful? Not in God's eyes. "My best days are behind me," some people say. That's not true if you are applying your faith in "all diligence," as we read in 2 Peter 1:5, (KJV). Applying your faith in all diligence brings you something that has nothing to do with age: moral excellence, knowledge, self-control, perseverance, godliness, brotherly kindness, and Christian love. And if these qualities are yours and are increasing (and they will be if your trust and faith is increasing), then they make you neither useless nor unfruitful.

There is a temptation to say, "I put in my time. I taught Sunday School. I served on the church board. I was camp superintendent. Now I'm retired. Let the younger ones do it. It's their turn." But when we say that, we've forgotten something. Young people may have more energy, but they don't have more experience. God has been preparing us for this time of life. All our lives God has been teaching us. It's like planting and cultivating through the late spring and the summer. Now it's harvest time, the best time of all. It certainly isn't just a time of getting ready for our final rest; that will come anyway, when God is ready.

Donald Sension, who was Director of Research Evaluation and Information Systems for the Hopkins, Minnesota school system, says, "Thirty years ago we talked about Christian ministry, but that's not the way things developed. Now, with retirement from the school system, I have the opportunity to do something different."

While he was still employed, he began getting his credentials in order. He and his wife sold their house and moved into an apartment to be freer to follow God's leading.

Some health problems Donald's wife has might limit where they can go and how much they can offer of themselves. He is open to teaching in Christian colleges and they are getting ready. God can work with that.

Am I Faithful?

Every one of us who claims to be a believer in Christ has a ministry ordained by God. Some are called to special forms of ministry, but all of us who are redeemed are ministers.

The Apostle Paul told young Timothy, "I thank Christ Jesus our Lord, who has given me strength, that he considered me faithful, appointing me to his service" (1 Timothy 1:12). You can turn that verse around and read it from the other direction too, "God put me into service or ministry because He counted me faithful." You may say, "I don't have a ministry or a place of service." Well, are you faithful?

Our Lord puts us into ministry or service as He counts us faithful. Paul says, "I thank Christ Jesus our Lord, who has given me strength" or enabled me. Are you enabled? Our Lord wants to enable you. Are you in ministry or service? He has called you to it. The question is not so much about ministry or service or even about His enabling, but, "Does the Lord count me among the faithful?"

Every one of us who says, "I belong to Christ," needs to ask, "Does my Lord count me faithful?"

We Don't Pack It In

We may leave our careers at a certain age, but because we are in Christ we don't retire. Christians don't assume that at sixty-five or seventy we wrap it all up and pack it in. We don't. We start building on the foundation that we've been laying all those years.

When a builder has put in a good foundation, he is really just getting started. In fact, the foundation will probably be the hidden part. What is about to be done next is the part that will be seen. That may be true in your life. And the need for ministry is not just in your immediate community or city. As the Gospel spreads in Latin America, Africa, Asia, and the former Soviet Union, we see people coming to Christ in numbers even exceeding the growth of the population. These churches and new believers, these Bible schools and mission centers need our help.

Recently, while in the former Soviet Union, I was interviewing Christians from many of the republics and I was impressed by the open doors. For however long it lasts, people can preach the Gospel in prisons, in hospitals, on the streets, in military installations, and even in public schools.

God is doing a new thing. In Revelation 21:5 we read, "He who was seated on the throne said, 'I am making everything new!' " And if ever there is an example of newness, it's there in the Eastern bloc countries. God opened it up as no human being could have done. A once atheistic group of nations now is hearing the Gospel and people are turning to Christ in great numbers— in fact, in some places faster than the church can absorb them, with increasing numbers of baptisms every month.

If God can do a new thing in places where we least

expected it, can't God also do a new thing in people's lives, even where we live? Maybe God is ready to do a new thing in your life, or for someone for whom you've been praying, and this is the day He is going to start.

With Our Own Peers

For us, especially if we are liberated from the old and are alert to the opportunities in the new situations in which God has placed us, one of those ministry opportunities may be with our own peers. Many people our own age have spent their lives rejecting Christ. But coming to later years, they are recognizing that their job didn't fulfill them, that the accumulation of money and things didn't satisfy, that the prestige and pleasures are all meaningless or vanity, as the writer of Ecclesiastes put it.

This age group is a ripe mission field. Who will go to them? Teenagers? People in their twenties and thirties and forties? Not likely. We are the missionaries to our peers, even as we are teachers to those coming along behind us. We have ministries in both directions.

A pastor whose primary ministry is to senior adults was talking about older people placing their faith in Jesus Christ. Many of them, hearing the Gospel in their seventies or eighties, have replied with words like, "That's the way I understood it when I was a child." They heard the Gospel, then rejected it for any number of reasons, and never came back to it until their years were nearly spent.

God is still offering salvation to people, and He always will. But for God to use us as late-in-life evangelists, we need to be growing—spiritually, emotionally, even academically. Sharp people are sharp witnesses.

This means we're alert to people and what they are

saying. We are alert to what is being published; we read prolifically, making that a part of our discipline. We take classes. We even take new part-time work opportunities.

Retirement isn't quitting; rather, it is going into other new phases of ministry, activity, or service. You say, "Well, I haven't got anything more to learn. I've seen it all." No, you haven't. There is more. And because God is in it, there may be much, much more.

The Apostle Paul summarized this in 1 Corinthians 2:9, "No eye has seen, no ear has heard, no mind has conceived what God has prepared for those who love him." That may be the word that describes your best years of evangelistic harvesting, beginning with people your own age.

But I've Had a Hard Life

Some say, "I can't serve God; I'm hurting. I can't imagine how anything good can come out of the problems I'm facing." Or they say, "My situation is hopeless; I see no value in what is happening. If only I could hear some good news." Well, your eye hasn't seen, your ear hasn't heard, and your mind can't even conceive—because your mind can work only with what is—what God has prepared. You can't even imagine what God has prepared for those who love Him. If you love Him, that promise is for you.

You and I don't have to try to figure out the reasons for all the unexpected things that come along in our lives. All we need to do is to continue to love God and wait to see what God is preparing for us. We know that whatever God is preparing for us is new. We haven't seen it before; we have never even heard of it; our minds can't even conceive it. But God has prepared it and it is for those who love Him.

"But I've had a hard life," you say. "I'm ill and home-bound. I'm in bed much of the time."

So you've got a lot of miles on you; maybe you're close to the end of your life's journey. Don't leave without one more investment of yourself, whatever it is—in a child's life, the life of a young parent, or another older person facing illness.

I have met people who are "old." Nobody else's problems are anywhere near as severe as theirs, no one's illness as bad as theirs, and every comment about the suffering of others brings them back to themselves and how much more they suffer. They're no pleasure to be around.

But I've met others who, because of the experience of their illness and pain, are growing. They are able to reach out and give comfort to people who are experiencing pain. They are bringers of good cheer and hope and life, even as they are dying themselves. They haven't slowed down just because of their own pain; they're still growing and giving, and they will continue to give of themselves right on to the end.

Building on What We Have

Long before we retire we make a decision about how we're going to live our remaining years. We decide the attitude we're going to have and the message we're going to proclaim. Then we keep bolstering that decision again and again with each passing day that God gives us. And someday, whether we're sixty-five or ninety-five, we will be able to say, "I'm still going on. There is still a contribution for me to make. God hasn't taken me home yet. I'm still growing."

Not long ago I sat with a group at the University of Minnesota's Hubert Humphrey Institute of Public Affairs. Our focus was on the major benefits of mid-career educational opportunities, which moved us into discussing end-of-career educational opportunities. The point made was that people who never had a chance for an education are finding that colleges are eager to have them. Retirees are going to college, some for the first time, taking courses they didn't have time to take before, stretching their minds in the classroom with younger people, participating in the give-and-take. Others who already have a college degree are doing graduate work in a specialty field that has captured their interest. "What's the practical aspect of that?" some might ask. "I'm too old to take a job in that field." That isn't the point. Education is for the sake of education—to grow, to stretch, to learn, to think.

People who go to college for the joy of learning study history or psychology or music or art to stretch their minds, to try new things, to meet new people. Many retirement communities are springing up in university and college towns because that's where the action is, that's where thinking is going on, plus there is the benefit of concerts and plays and guest lectures. Visit any YMCA and you'll find seventy-year-olds playing racquetball, running on the track, working the weight machines—people in great shape building on what they have. We continue to grow mentally, intellectually, and physically—if we want to.

Ours is a lifetime training program. That's what keeps us fresh. We are always able to learn, and because we do, we have more to teach.

When I was a seminary student, the teacher who influenced me the most was Dr. William E. Powers. Dr.

Powers didn't earn his Ph.D. until he was sixty and he was much older than that when he was my teacher. What an influence he had on me and every other student in that theological seminary! What if he had thought, "Age sixty is too old to get a doctorate"? So many lives have been changed over the years because we who were influenced by Dr. Powers have in turn influenced others, who in turn have influenced still others. Dr. Powers is long in heaven, but the impact of his life and teaching continues.

God's People Will Keep Going

If you read Galatians 5:7, you will find a quizzical Apostle Paul, "You were running a good race. Who cut in on you and kept you from obeying the truth?" Who hindered you? He is not asking what happened. He knows what happened—you started out well, but you are not doing well now. Somebody is hindering you. You know who that somebody is, don't you? Satan hinders you, but he can't stop you from obeying the truth if you want to. He can put up roadblocks, but you can go around them.

The Apostle Paul brings us face to face with a common spiritual problem. You were doing so well, but now you are not. Who hindered you from obeying the truth? "That kind of persuasion does not come from the one who calls you" (v. 8). God doesn't want you to stop. You were running so well, and you still can, you know, if you really want to. If you were doing well at age forty, keep on doing well at eighty.

God's people will grow. God's church will expand. God will work through His people and His church. If we isolate ourselves from the working of God because we are "too old," because we're "retired," we suffer, society suffers, and the kingdom suffers.

Am I growing yet? Am I on board with what God is doing now, today? The fields of God will have a harvest; will I be part of it?

Was I part of yesterday's blaze but today's cold ember? If I've dropped out of the fire, should I be praying, "God, throw me back in and let me burn well"? A lot of people, even those who for a while were out of the race, are getting back in.

Timothy Starr of Guelph, Ontario retired in 1989. "I was National Director of church planting and church growth in our denomination. I discovered that there were 14,000 seniors in our Ontario churches. I thought, 'How can I reach 14,000?' I felt we needed a publication, so we started *Link*. Within four months we had our first publication, and it has been going very well since.

"Seniors like traveling together. It's not that hard to put together a seniors' trip. And we also have builders who help us construct church buildings in Ontario and Quebec. We have also developed drama teams. People need to be given an opportunity to serve and to see others serving. In *Link* we publish what others are doing, to show people the possibilities. I'm an active person. I can't see myself sitting down. If the Lord spares me I'd hope for another five or six active years."

Building on Prayer

One evening I was in an hour-long prayer meeting. It was a very special time as we prayed together in small groups. A wonderful binding of hearts takes place when we are focused on the living Christ and sense the power of God's Holy Spirit helping us to pray. As Paul explained in Romans 12:15-16, we found we could "rejoice with those who rejoice; mourn with those who mourn. Live in harmony with one another." There is a wonderful coming together and a oneness in prayer that is not found in anything else we do.

When was the last time you were in a prayer group like that? If you're not in such a group, do you know what you are missing? Find one or start one. When you have a person or a group with whom you can pray, you will have an awareness of the power and the strength and the love and the peace of God that you will find in no other situation. Some very active Christians involved in the work of the church have missed that. For all their work they come away empty. But, oh, if they would pray, they'd come away full. Many older Christians have learned the value of prayer and have the time to pray for themselves and for each other. Whom do you know who would like to be full again? Invite that person to meet with you to pray.

Maybe you've never experienced anything as difficult as what you're experiencing right now. Maybe you're not sure you can make it. That shows that you're ready for what God is going to do as you pray. That's why, even if you never did much praying before, it's time to develop a life of prayer.

Are you under stress? Give that to God too. Make that the reason to call others to pray with you. One day, as part of a program for staying healthy, I was scheduled to take a stress test. When I arrived at the doctor's office and gave my name to the receptionist, she turned and yelled to a nurse, "Your stress is here." I laughed, and then wondered how many other people have said or thought when I have walked into a room, "Your stress is here."

That was on my mind during my devotions the next morning when I was reading from the Book of Esther. She must have been under tremendous stress. She was the only one in a position to deliver her people from sure annihilation. Yet, in spite of all that stress, she had to appear smiling and happy and please the king. "The king was attracted to Esther more than to any of the other women, and she won his favor" (Esther 2:17). He made her queen, and she did save her people. That would never have happened if, because of her own stress, it was announced to the king, "Your stress is here." He would not have loved Esther if she had brought her stress to him.

Burying stress is unhealthy. But there is a way of dealing with stress, and Esther knew what it was. She was a woman of God, a woman of obedience. She would have known, as every believer knows, that God is our refuge, our strength, our help in times of difficulty and trouble. She was a woman of prayer.

When you are under stress, give it to God, and He will help you with it. It will never be announced or even thought of when you enter a room, "Here comes our stress."

Some people say, "I don't want to serve anymore. I want to play." I've known people who retired to play and have been miserable because their play didn't satisfy. But I know others who have seriously prayed about their remaining years of life and have found new pleasures in their own usefulness. Are you growing yet as a man or woman of prayer? That's when real maturity comes.

As Dr. Henry Petkau prayed about his life and ministry in retirement, God led him wonderfully. He retired in 1985 from Brock University, St. Catharines, Ontario where he was an associate professor in educational psychology, with a Ph.D. in perceptual psychology.

"A church on the West Coast was going through a conflict and the pastors resigned. The church felt I could help them. So I retired and we moved to British Columbia where I helped the church for three years through reconciliation and restoration. When we felt we could leave the church on a good platform, we left. But we had no plans."

However, Dr. and Mrs. Petkau prayed some more. "Then the president of the Mennonite Brethren Bible College in Winnipeg called. Their business manager had resigned, and since I also have a master's degree in administration, we went there for two years. When the school moved to a liberal arts program, it was a good time to leave.

"We were ready to go back to Ontario when a church in Kitchener, Ontario called us. So we went there for a year to help them. They were without a pastor.

"As we were completing that, a large church in St. Catharines was having difficulty because the pastor had a serious heart attack. That sojourn took ten months.

"The precise timing of the Lord in all this is almost mind-boggling. Almost to the day sometimes, when one ministry ended, we were invited to a new one. Each leading of God was a step to what I did next. It spurs me on."

We don't stop growing when we retire. Like Dr. Petkau, if we are praying, we may find that we're just getting ready for the next step.

My Journey Isn't Over

The psalmist said that we will be "like a tree planted by streams of water, which yields its fruit in season and whose leaf does not wither" (Psalm 1:3). This is still our season. So we keep going on, letting God do what He does so well—restore our souls.

Scripture tells us not to grow weary in well-doing, but we do. We get worn out and even burned out. Yet, "he restores my soul. He guides me in paths of righteousness for his name's sake" (Psalm 23:3). Day by day, as we try to follow God in the paths of righteousness, we get hurt; we feel battered; sometimes the joy seems to leave us, but God doesn't leave us! As He guides us "in paths of righteousness for his name's sake," He will restore our souls—again, and again, and again.

Life may be long for you already, but your journey isn't over. Not yet. So keep looking to God for His leading. Henry Ward Beecher wrote,

> O Impatient Ones! Do the leaves say nothing to you as they murmur today? They are not fashioned this spring, but months ago; and the summer just begun will fashion others for another year. At the bottom of every leaf-stem is a cradle, and in it is an infant germ; and the winds will rock it, and the birds will sing to it all summer long, and next season it will unfold. So God is working for you and carrying forward to the perfect development all the processes of our lives.[1]

Your journey isn't over. If earlier you missed the works of God in your life, then seek them now. You may win your biggest battles yet. You may go home with great victories. Caleb did, and he was eighty-five. (See Joshua 14.)

As long as you have life remaining, commit yourself to be available for what God wants to do through you.

When God described David, He said, "He will do everything I want him to do." The Apostle Paul used that as a sermon illustration. "After removing Saul, He made David their king. He testified concerning him, 'I have found David son of Jesse a man after my own heart; he will do everything I want him to do' " (Acts 13:22).

Will God say that of me? Will God say that of you? God isn't finished with us yet. If He had finished with us, we'd be in heaven now. But we're still here. Therefore, we have to wonder what extraordinary thing God is yet going to do.

For Reflection:

1. What are you doing today to grow spiritually and intellectually?

2. What are you doing to improve your physical and emotional health?

3. What new work do you think God is even now preparing for you?

4. In your praying, regardless of your limitations, how are you making yourself available to God in new ways?

5. As you look ahead in your life journey, what do you think would be the best thing you could do? Go for it!

My Heritage, My Roots

10

*"The most important events in every age
never reach the history books."*
C.S. Lewis

*"To live well in the quiet routine of life,
to fill a little space because God wills it . . .
his works will follow him. He is one of God's heroes."*
Frederick William Farrar

While teaching at a writers' conference in Colorado, I was trying to make the point that writers cannot assume any residual Christianity in their readers. As I was talking, a woman at the back of the room raised her hand and said, "I'll give you an example of that." She said a friend went into a jewelry store to buy a cross for his teenage daughter to wear around her neck. The young woman behind the counter said, "Crosses? Oh, yes, we have two kinds. We have a plain one and we have one with a little man on it."

To people over fifty, this is shocking. To many people under fifty, it is not surprising at all. Conversations with boomers and busters, and articles and books about those generations, reveal not only a fluidity of conviction but a lack of biblical understanding. People over fifty are well aware that in their own years of formulating belief they pretty much knew what they believed by age twenty-five or thirty, and in the years following they built on that. We always thought that young people were best reached with the good news of the Gospel before age eighteen, because that was true for us. If people tended to be unbelievers at age twenty-five or thirty, we assumed that they would likely remain that way, short of the radical intervention of God in unique experiences—such as seen in the conversions of Malcolm Muggeridge, Chuck Colson, and Fred Barnes.

But that is no longer true. In an age when so many choices are available, in a generation with a supermarket or cafeteria mentality about philosophy, politics, and religion, there tends to be an unwillingness to make a firm commitment to anything. This means that a person at forty-five may be just as fluid in his religious beliefs or lack of them as seventeen- and eighteen-year-olds used to be. And when we drop down to the twenty-some-things, we have people who not only are fluid in their beliefs but have little teaching on which to base those beliefs, unless they and their parents are among those who are called by researchers, "the never lefts," those who never left the church.

But this fluid attitude does not necessarily mean anger toward or hatred of spiritual things. In fact, we are living in an age of spirituality, a looking beyond the scientific to the miraculous, past the known to the mystical. The desire to explore Eastern religions, and absorb New Age teachings in business and education, shows the hunger that people have, the desire for spirituality, though not necessarily a desire for God. People want to have roots.

Rootlessness

Rootlessness is real, and this rootless confusion regarding who God is, who we are, and how we can have security and peace permeates our culture. We say, "Why don't they commit themselves to Christ and the church?" One reason is that commitment is exactly what they do not want—not to organizations, not to ideas, sometimes not even to a marriage partner. Yet there is still the desire to belong, to know who they are and where they stand with God.

All around us people are on a spiritual quest looking for God, but mostly looking for God within themselves. They want to belong, but on their own terms. They desire security, but they want personal freedom too.

So many are wondering, "Where are my roots? Where do I belong? What did my parents and grandparents have that I don't seem to have?" They will not find the answer through the media, because most of the media tends to see Christians as narrow and bigoted, especially those who believe in the essentials of the faith. Christians are people to be mocked and criticized. Christians are even declared to be the destroyers of all that is good, ecologically, sociologically, and politically. For many in our society, Christians are the enemy.

But seekers are not necessarily controlled by the media. They understand selective news editing and they discount advertising hype. If for years they didn't want to believe what they were taught by those who loved them, neither do they want to believe what they are taught by those who don't. And though the influence of media is always great, it cannot block the thinking of an inquiring and searching person. An anti-Christian culture offers an opportunity for the Gospel.

We and our reactions to what is happening, we and our beliefs, we and our biblical roots, are being observed. We can learn how to show the power of God in our lives to our culture by copying the believers who went before us, those who were faithful to God in their culture.

Our forebears weren't just laughed at or mocked for their faith. That was only the mild part. Scripture says,

> Some faced jeers and flogging, while still others were chained and put in prison. They were stoned; they were sawed in two; they were put to death by the sword. They went about in sheepskins and goatskins, destitute, persecuted, and mistreated. . . . They wandered in deserts and mountains, and in caves and holes in the ground (Hebrews 11:36-38).

That's what it was to be a Christian then. But in the middle of that whole description there is a line that reads, "The world was not worthy of them." That's what we need to have in our minds. People of whom the world is not worthy may be subject to battering.

In our day, we are to remain faithful, a people approved. We are never to do anything on a human level to cause anger or disdain. But if anger comes because we are faithful to God and His truth, we can say, "Let it come." We are an example of another way, a better way.

A Heritage to Offer

We who have a heritage and an understanding of our roots have something to offer those coming along behind us. Cicero once said, "Not to know what happened before one was born is always to be a child." If we live only in the now, as a child does, if we are centered only on ourselves as in "What does this mean for me?" we are victims of our ignorance. We have no bigger picture, no scope by which to analyze, measure, assess, understand. All that is important didn't start with me, nor will it end with me. As a believer I am one part of God's whole picture.

Scripture gives us a wonderful sense of our roots and provides a balance to our lives. Take away that sense of identity and belonging and we will be pushed around by contemporary issues and thought. Take away those roots and we have neither perspective nor good footing. The best we can do is to pool our experiences with others and prop one another up as victims of the same difficulties.

History is God's story, but our educators have made it man's story. As a result, many remain as Cicero's child. In a society of children, biblically astute persons are adults and they are needed.

As rooted believers in Christ, we are what others are looking for. We have a great heritage to pass along. Ours is a great calling. Hebrews 11 lists those who went before us and lived by faith—Abraham, Isaac, Jacob, Moses, and others. They are our examples.

As we read the conclusion to that roll call of faith, we find ourselves listed too, "Therefore, since we are surrounded by such a great cloud of witnesses . . . let us run with perseverance the race marked out for us" (Hebrews 12:1).

They are there, those witnesses, cheering us on. We aren't in this battle alone. We aren't the first ones to run this race. Others have gone before us and they were faithful.

It's Our Turn Now

Now it's our turn. We fix our eyes on Jesus and "run with perseverance." That doesn't mean we have to be flashy or draw attention to ourselves or finish first. That doesn't mean we are even strong. It means *we will keep going*, as those before us kept going. As William Carey, that great pioneer missionary expressed it, "I can plod."

And how do we do that? We "fix our eyes on Jesus" (v. 2). We don't look this way or that to see who is noticing or cheering. We don't look for a way out or a shorter route. We go the distance with our eyes locked on Jesus Christ, the One for whom we run this race.

Don't grow weary or lose heart. In your running, in your persevering, "you have not yet resisted"—as so many others have had to resist—"to the point of shedding your blood" (v. 4). You might be one of the martyrs, but not yet. Keep going.

We'd never make it if we had only ourselves and our own resources. But we have what those others had who went before us. We have what faithful Christians have had for generations—perseverance, no matter what happens, be it illness or financial setbacks. Like them, we have our eyes fixed on one Person, the One who called us, the One who saved us, the Lord Jesus Christ.

Some of us become too self-assured as we live the Christian life. We begin to assume that we are quite valuable, that maybe the church couldn't get along so well without us, that we are the ultimate wisdom in our church board meetings, that our theology is far deeper and more true to Scripture than anybody else's.

That kind of pride is a creeping thing. We forget that we are branches, that our Lord is the vine. As Paul put it, "You do not support the root, but the root supports you" (Romans 11:18). He was talking about the grafted Gentile church being arrogant toward the original branches, the Israelites. He said, "You do not support the root, but the root supports you." If we could keep remembering that, it would make a lot of difference in the way we behave toward one another in the church and in how we pass on the faith to others.

It is because they were rooted that our forefathers could fight and win the heresy battles. It is because they were rooted that missions were founded. It is because they were rooted that they could build abolitionist societies and free the slaves. Because they were rooted they could care for those who were hurting, build hospitals and orphanages and homes for older people. It was those rooted in the faith who built so many universities.

It is those who are rooted in faith who make society better. The more we are in touch with our roots, the more we'll realize our rich heritage, where we've come from, and our part in adding to the great work of God.

Enlarged Faith

If the church is a divine institution (and it is), if we are redeemed members of the Body of Christ (and we are), if Christ is the Head (and He is), and if the Holy Spirit is the One who gives gifts for the building of the church so that it can grow (and He does), then that gives a lot of meaning to what Paul is talking about in Ephesians 2:10 when he says, "For we are God's workmanship, created in Christ Jesus to do good works, which God prepared in advance for us to do."

We are part of that holy, living church attached to Him, and we are His workmanship—put here for good works. If you are a believer, don't ever think of yourself as just a person who goes to church. If you are a believer, God is working in you as part of His church to make it vibrant, alive, growing, and powerful. If you ever cut yourself off from that, you'll also cut yourself off from all that He intended you to be.

A lot of people who claim to be Bible-believing Christians don't have fellowship with the Christian church. That's like saying, "I am part of the body, but I am not attached to the body," or "I am one of the branches of the vine, but I am not attached to the vine." And that is probably the reason why these same people are seen to be slipping more and more spiritually. Measured against themselves, they are quite content with their spiritual state. But measured by other believers, it is obvious that the more they are alone, the less they are walking with the Savior.

That is what Paul was referring to in 2 Thessalonians 1:3, "We ought always to thank God for you, brothers, and rightly so, because your faith is growing more and more, and the love every one of you has for each other is increasing." As they loved one another, their faith was enlarged. When we have a relationship with other believers, iron sharpens iron, one teaches another, we are encouraged, we are edified and brought along. As Paul said, we are "growing more and more" or are "greatly enlarged." Our love for one another enlarges our faith. This enlarged faith causes us to love one another all the more.

Accountable?

Am I in touch with my roots? Am I an example of the committed believer? Am I accountable? Am I dependable?

Cafeteria-type Christians lose a sense of accountability. They don't want to be committed to a local church but go here, go there, sample a little bit of this and that. "If the sermon is good down the street, that is where we will go on Sunday. If something else is happening, like a concert, that is where we will go." They like what they like, served the way they like it served; and if it doesn't please them, they go elsewhere. They have no commitment, no service, and no accountability. In time, they begin to grow cold and dry up, even wither and die.

Nehemiah gives us a good example of people who are committed to each other. It's the description of people standing guard. He said, "Appoint residents of Jerusalem as guards, some at their posts and some near their own houses" (Nehemiah 7:3).

When a person belongs somewhere, he is far more accountable. When he has a house, a family, it is more likely that he can be depended on. Not so the one who says, "I will guard if I feel like it, where I feel like it, when I feel like it, and wherever the shade is better." He is not dependable. But the guard in front of his own house, like the person in the local church, knows the people in that house. He is accountable to the people in that house. And they are accountable to him. He has a commitment.

We have a need for people to stand guard, to present the truth, to wear the armor of God, to help one another, to stand side by side being accountable. There may be cafeteria people drifting around, supermarket people selecting a place to stand for a little while, but they are not dependable because they are not accountable.

Are you accountable to a local body of believers? Can you be depended upon to be there, to take your place, to make your contribution?

We are told to stimulate or build up one another to love and good deeds—to help people and also to be helped. Scripture instructs us, "Let us not give up meeting together, as some are in the habit of doing, but let us encourage one another" (Hebrews 10:25).

Don't Cheat Yourself

If we don't gather to be taught, if we don't gather to be used of God with our gifts for the sake of others, then we are like the hand saying to the foot, "I don't need you," or the eye to the ear, "I have no need of you." That's what is happening with so many who are wanting to practice individualistic faith and to ignore the body of believers. God never intended that and He doesn't want it. He says we are to "encourage one another—and all the more as you see the Day approaching" (Hebrews 10:25).

Don't forsake the assembling of yourselves together, we are told. If we do, we will cheat the church. We will cheat ourselves. We will cheat God.

What a heritage we have as Christian believers, and what a sadness that not all Christians pay much attention to their heritage. If we don't know the struggles of those who went before, we won't know of the wonderful power of God available to us today.

Psalm 22:4 says, "In you our fathers put their trust; they trusted and you delivered them." Church history shows us that even when a person dies a martyr, God brings great deliverance. We only have to look at Stephen and realize what his dying witness was to Saul of Tarsus who became the Apostle Paul, the greatest missionary of all time.

We need more books written on missionary leaders;

retired persons could write those books. We need to alert more people to our heritage, our church history, especially when we live in a time when many people think that history begins and ends with them.

A Gift of Myself

It is the body of Christ, the church, that is going to challenge and change culture. A changed culture can change politics, especially in a democracy where politics reflects culture. The church, the body of believers, is leaven to our culture; as yeast, it permeates—if it hasn't lost its yeastiness. The body has the Spirit, and there's no limit to the influence on culture that the Spirit-led church can have. Then a changed culture brings a changed society.

We are not retired from life. Therefore our greatest influence on people and culture may still be ahead. In Christ we have a power that can change thinking. We are ballast in a ship that is listing first this way and then that way in storm-tossed seas. We are rooted while living in an increasingly rootless culture. We are responsible, accountable, solid demonstrations of what it means to belong to God.

And how do we show it? We can show it to others gathered around our own firesides. C.S. Lewis said, "Dyson and Tolkien were the immediate human causes of my conversion. Is any pleasure on earth as great as a circle of Christian friends by a good fire?"[1]

We can show it in what we leave behind for others. Recently a friend took his video camera on a visit to his father who is in his nineties. As his father spoke about his roots, family history, beliefs, and trust in God, the video was recording. It has been shown at family gatherings, watched by individuals two and three generations down the line. The stories are retold with each showing of that video.

We can tell what we believe on audiotapes. How many elderly people have had the privilege of speaking into a cassette recorder and relating for all who will come after them the history of the family and of the family's faith? They are the proof that God is faithful in good times and in bad, that when all was dark God kept His word. Their stories give continuity. They show what is important, what is lasting, and what is changing.

Recently a woman sent me a book of poems about her life, her conversion and beliefs, her roots in Christ. She hoped there was a market for them. There is little market for poetry, but there is something better. I told her, "Have some copies made, bind them in a folder, and give them as gifts to your extended family. Let them cherish what you wrote for generations to come. This is your heritage, a gift of yourself."

More and more people are writing their family history. There are writers in most families who will help older people do that—a niece, a cousin, a grandson. When those stories are printed and bound, generations to come will see that we were who we were not because we were unusual, but because we were rooted in Christ Jesus.

We are part of ongoing church history. We are proof that the work of God didn't end with the Reformation or with the beginning of the missionary movement. It continues, and we are part of that great movement.

Check Your Life, Check Your Witness

Do not let your personal wants or the suffering of your last years be your permanent heritage to others, for God has been much bigger to you than some immediate pain. Determine not to let illness or pain make you a complainer. Do not attack others, even if they have hurt you; do not attack the church which nurtured you.

Lately I have heard some terrible stories—of people attacking their pastors until they have left the ministry, of church members going to court against fellow members. I place that which I am hearing against what I read in God's Word.

Paul told Titus, "Remind the people to be subject to rulers and authorities, to be obedient, to be ready to do whatever is good" (Titus 3:1). Be ready for every good deed. If you are ready for every good deed, you will not pounce on everything that you think is wrong or done against you.

Paul went on, "Be ready to do whatever is good, to slander no one, to be peaceable and considerate, and to show true humility toward all men." Then he showed the contrast, "At one time [that is, before we were saved, before we were in Christ, before we knew God's grace, before we knew the love of God flowing into us] we too were foolish, disobedient, deceived and enslaved by all kinds of passions and pleasures. We lived in malice and envy, being hated and hating one another" (vv. 2-3).

When we are critical, our actions and our words betray the faith we once declared. It is just as if Christ had never come, as if salvation had never occurred, as if the love of God had not filled us. Yet, Paul continued, "But when the kindness and love of God our Savior appeared, he saved us" (vv. 4-5).

We are washed. We have the Holy Spirit renewing us. We have roots in the living Christ, and our heritage for others is our strong faith in Him. When Polycarp was martyred at the stake, he said, "Eighty-six years I have served Him, and He has done me no wrong. How can I blaspheme my King who has saved me?" He couldn't, he wouldn't, and we are not to deny Him or say blasphemous things at the end of our lives either.

A lot of people are talking about the soon return of the Lord. Certainly His coming again is nearer than it was a day ago, last month, or a thousand years ago. But we are not to be just standing around waiting for Him. What's our responsibility while we wait for the return of the Lord? We are told in the First Epistle to Timothy how to behave. For we are the church, the redeemed, the ones for whom Christ is returning. We are the people of God, built on God's Word, which is His truth, nurtured by the guiding, filling Holy Spirit; and our responsibility in the days between now and when Christ comes again is to hold up to the world the truth of God's Word.

Paul said to Timothy that the house of God is the church of the Living God, the pillar and ground of the Truth. If that is so, then that's what we are to live by, that's what guides everything that we do, and that's what we proclaim to the world.

How are you doing with Christ? Check your life, check your witness. Be sure that having run well with Christ you also finish well. Others will see—people do watch us.

Seeing the Goodness

I was thinking about Gehazi, a man whose story is recorded in 2 Kings. Although Gehazi did some things that were wrong, he is remembered because he was Elisha's servant. One day the king said to Gehazi, "Tell me about all the great things Elisha has done" (2 Kings 8:4), so he did.

In many ways that's what we all do. We're not necessarily involved in great things, but we see many acts of
God as they are performed through other people. When
Elisha restored a woman's son to life, Gehazi saw that
and told about it. He wasn't involved but he was a teller.

Isn't that what we're doing? We tell about God's great
acts. I may not be preaching on Sunday, but I see the
results of a good sermon and I tell about it. I may not be
teaching, but I see the results of that teaching and I tell
about it. "Look at what God has done," I say.

It is good to be alert to what God is doing through
other people. Sometimes we are too interested in looking at what God is doing through ourselves to see all the
mighty works of God being performed through other
believers as well. It enlarges our vision when we begin
to watch for ways that God is working through others,
and it does us a lot of good to tell about it. We show that
we are truly a big family, and we let people know that
we belong to that wonderful family.

The Apostle Paul helps us here. He said, "Let us therefore make every effort to do what leads to peace and to
mutual edification. Do not destroy the work of God"
(Romans 14:19-20). We are in the business of building,
strengthening, encouraging, edifying, and helping the
body of Christ. And so we pursue the things that make
for peace and harmony. This doesn't mean we compro-
mise on essentials. It means that we focus on the kingdom and not on our own small opinions. When we focus
on what God is doing, we do not tear down the work of
God, but build it up.

There is a lot of work to be done as we serve our Lord
together. Let's always be certain that we are indeed doing it together.

If you have a wonderful Christian family heritage, or

if you're the only believer in your household, give glory to God. Point always to Him, so that with the psalmist you are able to say, "I am still confident of this: I will see the goodness of the Lord in the land of the living" (Psalm 27:13).

In understanding our own roots we know who we are in Christ. And knowing who we are, we can present with understanding the promises of God to others — promises that are for today, tomorrow, and forever.

That's our heritage to pass along. And, maybe, because we are faithful, that will be some other person's heritage too. Then, recalling you, he or she will say, "I remember my spiritual roots."

For Reflection:

1. Because most people today have little spiritual heritage, what are you doing to pass along the heritage you have?

2. Have you written, videotaped, or recorded on audiotape your spiritual heritage? It is a gift you need to give to others.

3. How are you helping your peers understand the rootlessness of so many young people? Are you showing that it is not a subject for criticism but a doorway to ministry?

4. We live in a rootless culture. How are you offering the roots that others need?

5. What heritage are you leaving upon which others may build their lives in Christ?

A Going-Away Party

11

"Good-bye, proud world! I'm going home."
Ralph Waldo Emerson

"God's finger touched him, and he slept."
Alfred, Lord Tennyson

Soon there will be a going-away party. It will be a celebration, a graduation party. A lot of people will be invited, and you might assume that you are the guest of honor because they are all coming to see you.

One day Jesus went to a wedding party held at Cana. A lot of people were there to celebrate with the bride and groom. But our Lord worked a miracle that day, turning water into wine. That evening when the guests went home they probably told their friends and neighbors about the bride and groom. But their chief topic of conversation was, "Jesus was there. Let me tell you what He did!"

The death of any believer is a celebration. We are

graduating from this life with all of its struggles and problems. After attempting to live as God would have us live, we now enter a time of rejoicing and praise, ready to hear those wonderful words, "Well done, good and faithful servant! . . . Come and share your master's happiness!" (Matthew 25:21)

Your death is going to be a celebration of all God is and all that He has done in your life. You need to be preparing for that going-away party even now.

We Won't Go Alone

There are some things about dying we don't know. We don't know what the process will be like. We don't know if it will hurt. We don't know if there will be darkness in the valley of the shadow of death. But some things are certain. We know that someday we will be in a place where there is no pain, no fear, no confusion, no emotional hurts, and that we will not go through that valley alone. It was C.S. Lewis who said:

> You needn't worry about not feeling brave. Our Lord didn't—see the scene in Gethsemane. How thankful I am that when God became man He did not choose to become a man of iron nerves; that would not have helped weaklings like you and me nearly so much.[1]

We will not go through our valley alone. We have the assurance, "You are with me" (Psalm 23:4).

I have never met Will Leff, but I have received correspondence from him through his wife, Carol. She is his interpreter, because a serious illness left him unable to speak. But he can pray, and that is why I admire him. When I walk through the valley, whether it is short or long, I'd like to face the valley as Will Leff is. He writes to his friends:

> I have learned experientially the truth of the Scripture that says, "Though I walk through the valley of the shadow of death I will fear no evil for Your rod and staff shall comfort me."
>
> God, for reasons only He knows, has granted me additional time here on earth, and I want to clearly know what He has for me to accomplish with whatever time I have remaining. Please pray I will hear Him clearly.
>
> I am keeping a list of all your names on the prayer board by my bed, and for the next few months I will be praying for you as the Lord leads.

Before being stricken with multiple sclerosis, Will was marketing manager for Martin Marietta, traveling the world for the aerospace giant. Now he has a prayer board next to his bed with pictures of people who have asked him to pray for them or their children. Although he is unable to speak clearly, he knows that God understands him when he prays.

Would he change anything about his life? He says not. "In my case, I must trust God and serve Him with whatever I can find to do."

Someday—The New Heaven

I have been reading about the new heaven, the holy city in the Book of Revelation. I like what I read there. For example, I read that we are going to see God's face and that there won't be any night.

Think of it—no stumbling around, no confusion, no longer wondering where we are going or what is ahead.

No night there, so we won't need a lamp. In other words, no artificial light. We won't even need the sun. Why? Because the Lord God shall illumine us, and we shall reign forever and ever. Think of it! Not only reigning but illuminated by God, in our thinking and feeling, illuminated in our worship, illuminated in every part of our being—lighted and really seeing. That is what it is going to be like. "When evening comes, there will be light" (Zechariah 14:7).

Some friends have suffered as I never have, those with incurable illnesses, those with terrible heartache, and those who have suffered their whole life long for their faith, persecuted because they are followers of Jesus. Personally, I have known none of that, and so it would be almost unkind for me to make a response to their pain with words such as, "Well, it won't be long before you are in heaven." But actually, Scripture has done that, not as a way of dismissing pain but as a way of recognizing it and the brevity of life, as well as the joy of eternal life in Christ and the crown that awaits us.

Revelation 2:10 says, "Do not be afraid of what you are about to suffer. I tell you, the devil will put some of you in prison to test you, and you will suffer persecution. . . . Be faithful, even to the point of death, and I will give you the crown of life."

"Be faithful, even to the point of death." Hold steady until you die. That is what our Lord is saying. And actually that is not a very long time to hold steady, not when we consider all of eternity. This is an encouraging word, not a word of casual dismissal of our pain. Hold on until death. Hold on until your coronation. The promise is there, "I will give you the crown of life." The Word of God puts into perspective the pain experienced by so many of God's people.

You May Not See All Your Victories

How long are we going to be around? None of us knows. The psalmist said, "My times are in your hands" (Psalm 31:15). There is a wonderful passage in 1 Peter that tells us our stay here on earth is temporary. And that's good to think about, because it causes us to live in respect, honor, and obedience to God. "Since you call on a Father who judges each man's work impartially, live your lives as strangers here in reverent fear" (1 Peter 1:17). Fear means awe, respect, and honor. We have a healthy understanding that God is judge, and we will honor Him as judge. We address Him as Father, the One who judges impartially.

For us tomorrow may not come. Ours is a temporary stay. Don't get caught by the idea that says, "Oh, I've got a long time," because you may not. But even if you do have a long time, honor the One you call Father.

Maybe you're saying, "I'm not ready to die yet. I haven't done all that I should have done. I haven't finished all that I want to accomplish." Don't you think God knows what you've done? If He's ready to take you home, then He must feel that you have done enough. Your life is complete if God is ready for you to go home.

Paul refers to people like us when he says, ". . . as you hold out the word of life—in order that I may boast on the day of Christ [that is, the day when Christ returns or the day when I meet Him face to face] that I did not run or labor for nothing" (Philippians 2:16).

You may not see all your victories. You may not know all that your faithfulness means to the larger body of believers. You may not know how your ministry is affecting the kingdom work. But if you are holding fast to the Word of Life, then what you do is not a waste of time and your life has had meaning. You are not running or toiling in vain. The faithful never do run in vain. What they do always counts.

Scripture tells us, "Precious in the sight of the Lord is the death of his saints" (Psalm 116:15). Those who believe are His saints, those who have been sanctified, made right through the sacrificial death of the Lord Jesus Christ on the cross and through His resurrection. Because He conquered death, He offers us life without the restrictions of death. "Whoever believes in the Son has eternal life. . . . Whoever believes in him shall not perish but have eternal life" (John 3:36, 16). That is a certainty. Second Timothy 4:18 assures us not only that He will rescue us but He will bring us "safely to his heavenly kingdom."

Not everyone is ready for the invitation to their going-away party, but that invitation is coming. We are going to die, and we have preparations to make.

Getting Ready

For many years my driver's license has carried the word "donor." That means if I should be killed, my organs can be given to other people. I want to know that even in my death I have offered life and meaning to somebody else. Perhaps the person who receives my heart or some other organ will be able to give many more years of faithful service to the King of kings. Think of it! That gift from me may enable the Gospel to be preached after I am gone. Or perhaps the recipient is not a believer, but during those years of added life will be receptive to an invitation to give his or her life to Jesus Christ as Savior and Lord.

But maybe I will die of old age with organs no longer

usable. Some Christians realize the value of allowing their bodies to be used for medical science research for future physicians to learn their craft and someday be able to save lives because of what they've learned from our bodies. Because of us, many doctors will be better able to save the lives of people who may someday be evangelists or missionaries or witnesses in their neighborhoods. They will train other doctors who will then save other lives in an ever-expanding pool of healing because initially some young physicians and surgeons learned their craft through the gift of our bodies to medical science. If this is your decision you need to fill out the necessary legal forms.

But you not only have a body with valuable organs or a body that can become a teaching tool. You also have property and financial resources to give. Have you a properly drawn will that spells out your wishes? You may think that you have such a small estate that you don't need a will, that your goods will automatically go to your spouse and children and other relatives. But if your will is not properly drawn, your wishes may be probated at a cost to your family.

You also need a living will or perhaps to select someone with durable power of attorney, because the process of dying is no longer as simple as it once was. Through medical technology your body may be kept alive longer than you want it to be. There's a lot of difference between hurrying death and not preventing the natural process of going home to heaven. We want to die when our time has come; few of us want to be kept alive after our minds have gone. Few of us want to create great medical costs for our families.

Have you designated someone who can make decisions for you if you are incapacitated? It is so much easier for family if they know their loved one has said, "This is what I want." It is so much better if it's in writing, so that in the grief of the moment the spouse, the children, and the other relatives can say, "This is exactly what he asked for. We are fulfilling his wishes. We are keeping faith with her desires." You can give your loved ones that peace of mind.

The memories of a total life lived and the victory of the homegoing needs to be seen as far more than the hanging on to one last minute of agonizing breath, especially if that minute is so costly, emotionally, physically, and financially. Have you prepared your advance directive so that family and physicians know exactly what you believe and want?

What a wonderful opportunity through your living will or your last will and testament to tell about your faith in Christ. You can say, "I believe that I am owned, body and soul, by God. Do not use mechanical means to prevent my soul, entombed in a physical body that no longer functions, from going to God." What a witness that is! And when your last will and testament is read, will people hear your testimony in the words of your will? Is there something there about how you lived trusting Jesus Christ as your Savior and Lord?

Eager people will hear your last will and testament. Let it be a real testament to your faith. They cannot hear you verbally any longer, but they can hear your words about what was so meaningful to you, words about trusting the Savior. Someone hearing your will read may realize that what really matters is not the money they might inherit, but eternal life which is the pearl of greatest price.

You can take the opportunity to tell the hearers, "I trusted Jesus Christ as my Savior and Lord. He said, 'I am come that they might have life and have it abundantly,' and I have found that absolutely true." You can even add, "I urge each person present at this reading to be certain that you also have new life in Christ. I want to meet all of you in heaven."

Besides your last will and testament and your living will, there are other bequests you need to make. Have you made a list of the gifts you want to give to specific friends and loved ones? Better yet, while you are still alive, experience the joy of giving to them what you want them to have. What a delight, when you know your own death is coming, to be able to say to a son or daughter or grandchild, "This is for you. I want you to have this because . . ." and then explain the significance of that gift.

As you plan your will, remember that as a believer you always gave at least a tithe of your income to Christian ministries and missions. Shouldn't you do the same now in your will? Are there missionary societies, or is there a church, to which at least 10 percent of your bequest should go? And isn't it a witness to those who hear the will read after you're gone that the first 10 percent, in keeping with your life practice, goes to the ministries listed? Then the remainder to the family members. Those who have never thought about the true value of investing in the kingdom will be very sensitive to it at that moment, and you may preach a better sermon about tithing than any pastor could.

Forgiving While You Can

Have you prepared for your death by setting straight bad accounts with others? Is there a need to repair broken relationships before you die? A need to mend fences?

Even though it should have been done sooner (we are told not to let the sun go down on our wrath), you can do it now. Through letters, phone calls, and personal visits, let people know that you are not going to live much longer. A fence was broken during your lifetime; you want to repair it while you are still alive.

Some people will refuse reconciliation. You can't force it, but you need to be the first to take the initiative. Jesus said, "Therefore, if you are offering your gift at the altar and there remember that your brother has something against you, leave your gift there in front of the altar. First go and be reconciled to your brother; then come and offer your gift" (Matthew 5:23-24). Don't wait for him to come to you.

Is God wanting to love that person through you and you're the block? Has the one who was so mean to you before changed with age? Is there something going on in that person's life now that makes him or her different? Will your desire to repair hurts be a step in the greater restoration process—restoration with God?

You may be hurt again through your efforts, as you open yourself and become vulnerable. But you have the Comforter with you; you have the Heavenly Father to turn to. You have the example of Jesus who "was despised and rejected by men" (Isaiah 53:3). He offered Himself for the world. "While we were still sinners, Christ died for us" (Romans 5:8). "Your attitude should be the same as that of Christ Jesus" (Philippians 2:5). You may be hurt, but you will have tried, and that's the mark of a mature believer.

Seeking reconciliation should not be done without much prayer for the mind and heart of God. But we know enough from God's Word that it is clear what we must do. "Bear with each other and forgive whatever grievances you may have against one another. Forgive as the Lord forgave you" (Colossians 3:13). Think about that! Jesus forgave me, so I am to forgive someone who has a quarrel with me (or I with him).

God had every right not to forgive me. There was nothing forgivable about me, nothing good about me, but the great heart of God opened to me in forgiveness. If then I have been forgiven that much, why will I not forgive another? I know some Christians who harbor grudges, who never forget a quarrel or a complaint against another, who know that they are going to have to spend eternity with that person, but don't want to make things right now.

When I put the two side by side—Christ's forgiveness of me and my forgiveness of another—my forgiving of that other person is as nothing compared to Christ forgiving me. He lives in me and He wants to love through me and forgive through me.

Are there people you need to forgive—people you need to talk to tonight or tomorrow? Isn't it time to do that?

Augustine spoke of "good death." Could forgiveness be part of the "good death" for us?

See How a Christian Dies

Your dying process may be short or long. Let people know what it is to die in Christ, to see how a Christian dies. Is there pain? Let them see how a Christian handles pain. Are there crippling effects? Let them see how a Christian handles that. We have all heard people say, "You don't know what I'm going through," and that's true. At the same time, we don't want to make what we're going through such a central part of our whole witness that people concentrate more on the pain of dying than on the victory at the other end. Show them who will sustain them by showing them who sustains you.

When we visit a hospital and try to comfort a patient, we don't tell them, "I know exactly how you feel," because we can never know what someone else is going through. But God knows. Even in our own last severe illness, God knows what we are going through. He knows our feelings, our pain, and our circumstances. The psalmist knew that God knew. That's why he could say in Psalm 55:22, "Cast your cares on the Lord and he will sustain you." The burden is there, and maybe God won't take it away; but we do have the assurance that He will sustain us.

What are you facing? He will sustain you. What's happening to you? He will sustain you. What burden is pressing you down? Cast that burden on the Lord, and He will sustain you. It's good news that we don't have to carry our burdens by ourselves.

Like many of us, David felt beaten down by life. It was overwhelming to him, but God brought him through. He didn't say, "Thanks for conquering my enemies." He didn't say, "Thanks for my victory." He said, "If the Lord had not been on our side ... the raging waters would have swept us away" (Psalm 124:1, 5). The point is that God was on his side and he wasn't overwhelmed; he didn't drown in his troubles.

"Praise be to the Lord," he said, "who has not let us be torn by their teeth. We have escaped like a bird out of the fowler's snare; the snare has been broken, and we have escaped" (vv. 6-7).

That is why this thought is so refreshing and different. The psalmist didn't blame God for his troubles; he didn't ask God to smash those who were hurting him. He gave thanks to God that in rough times God was there helping him through.

Going Home

You are going home. Perhaps you're getting close and your thoughts are leaning more and more in that direction.

You spent a lifetime looking forward to things you wanted—a new car, a trip to Europe, some new clothes. Now you are looking forward to heaven. So was Peter. He said, "We are looking forward to a new heaven and a new earth, the home of righteousness" (2 Peter 3:13).

Someday it will be announced, "He is gone" or "She's in heaven now." If you know the Lord, you'll be rejoicing—but others will be crying. That's natural. They did not want you to go.

Yet their tears will be mixed with excitement wondering, "What is he facing now?" "What is she experiencing?" "What kind of rejoicing is going on, as the angels sing a great welcome?" Let the joy you are experiencing be their joy at your death.

Are you ready for your going-away party? The one that will lead directly to your welcome-home party? Aren't you glad that your preparations are made? That your reservations are being held for you?

Don't you enjoy it when you go to a restaurant and there is a long line but you have reservations? Doesn't it feel good to have reserved seats at a sporting event? And aren't you much more relaxed flying with reservations rather than standby?

In Peter's epistle we read of an inheritance which is imperishable, undefiled, and will not fade away. It's reserved in heaven for you (1 Peter 1:4). A reserved inheritance that already has your name on it. It won't perish because it's imperishable. It won't be something defiled because it can't be defiled. It will not fade away. It will always be there. It's reserved.

And why is this inheritance reserved? We have a living hope through the resurrection of Jesus Christ from the dead, because according to His great mercy He has caused us to be born again (1 Peter 1:3). Peter wouldn't say it if God hadn't done it. A reservation in heaven! An inheritance—imperishable! Undefiled! Eternal! So relax. You've got a reservation.

Some people think they won't know until they get to the door whether or not they will enter heaven. You have the certain inheritance because you have trusted Christ Jesus. Now, your final ministry is to help other people understand this so they too can trust Christ Jesus and have the assurance of God's inheritance.

Until then we wait for the party—and the opening strains of the orchestral welcome.

I think it was the composer Franz Liszt who spoke about our lives being only a prelude, an overture, to the real symphony, the first note of which will be struck at our death. Think of it. We listen to the opening strains of music, and we anticipate the full orchestral beauty of the symphony.

Someday we will move past the beginning, past the prelude, past the overture, and when our friends are saying, "He is gone," we will have entered into a hall unlike any on earth for a symphony such as we have never heard before.

I am enjoying the overture now, but I am looking forward to the full symphony.

Going home! There is so much to look forward to.

For Reflection:

1. Some people tend to postpone preparing the legal papers that will be needed before and after death. Have you prepared all of yours?

2. Have you repaired any broken relationships? Are there any fences still not mended?

3. Are you beginning to give away those special gifts intended for particular loved ones?

4. Will the people gathered at your deathbed fully understand your faith in Christ? Are there any to whom you need to speak about it now?

5. Are you preparing to show others how a Christian dies? Are you praying to be faithful to the end?

Death Plus Five Years

12

"When I go down to the grave I can say, like so many others, I have finished my work; but I cannot say I have finished my life. My day's work will begin the next morning."
Victor Hugo

"So he passed over, and all the trumpets sounded for him on the other side."
John Bunyan

I am working on a speech that I must deliver in a few days. A speech is constructed like a building. We start with an outline, which is sort of like a blueprint, and then build the speech step by step, adding, sometimes subtracting, then completing it with finishing touches that include anecdotes, illustrations, and examples. It takes a long time to build a good speech, but the result is a memorable statement that causes changes in the hearers' lives.

As I am working on a speech, I wonder if God is also building me into a statement. Am I a message about His grace, His goodness, and His redemptive work? Some buildings, like some speeches, are poorly planned and poorly built. Sometimes they are covered over with cosmetic appeal that fools people but doesn't hold up. Some speeches are exciting on first hearing, but prove to have little lasting value. Is my life one of content? Or is it only show, a facade, an entertainment, with little of quality beneath?

A well-grounded speech is long remembered. A well-grounded Christian is long remembered also. Such a Christian is a statement about God.

What Will They Remember?

When I'm gone, what will people remember of me? Will they remember the hours I spent at work? Or the help that I gave to other people? What will people recall five and ten years after I'm gone? I will be part of that great cloud of witnesses who are praising God, but I will also be a legacy that is left behind.

What is left when I'm gone is what I've given to others. What I've given will never end. We are like messages to be recalled for years to come.

One day at a writers' conference a publisher praised two of my books. Afterward I went to her and said, "That was very kind of you, and I appreciate your words. But you know as well as I do that those books are out of print." She replied, "Books are never out of print. Somewhere those books exist. People have them on their bookshelves; they've passed the book along to a friend or neighbor. Someone in a younger generation has picked up that book to read. It is sold at a garage sale and a new person reads it. It's in libraries across the country." Then she emphasized again, "A book is never out of print." And I thought, *Our lives are like books—we're never out of print.*

Things people keep to remind them of you will last years after you're gone. The letter you sent to a grandchild won't be thrown away. Your marked Bible is being cherished by someone. The cards you sent to offer sympathy or cheer, or to remind someone that you were praying for them, are still being cherished. The audio or video from a birthday celebration so long ago is still being listened to or watched, and people are remembering. The words you said will not be forgotten.

Five years after your death, will letters that you wrote still be reread? Five years after your death, which birthday or Christmas gift will someone look at and remember? A Bible story book given to the children? A present to a grandchild who, now grown, recalls how special it was to receive that gift from you? Five years after your death what conversations will be remembered? Five years after your death who, learning that he has a death-threatening illness, will recall that you knew how to die? Will he think about the inner peace you had and remember why you had it?

Five years after your death, who will find a clipping from the obituary column or the folder from your funeral, or will make another visit to your graveside and remember—not just you but what you believed, what you stood for? What reflection will take place at that moment because for the first time a person's heart is ready for the message from your life?

Five years after your death, who will meet one of your children or grandchildren and ask, "Oh, are you related to. . . ?" and then tell them how years before you taught a Sunday School class that meant so much, or how you led a child to Christ, or how you helped that person with money when it was most needed, or visited when there was sickness in the home? God has a way of bringing the right person across someone's path at the right spiritual moment with the right recollection. And maybe it will be less than five years.

I remember my grandmother. I remember her Bible. I can see it still on the table by her chair, her glasses on top of it. I remember my dad and how he died, right there in church. I think about them and I remember.

People will draw on the treasures you leave behind. There is no end to the value of treasures when those treasures are from you. Especially the spiritual ones.

That Great Treasure

Anyone who has owned a piece of property for a length of time has seen its value fluctuate over the years. Anyone who has investments in stocks or bonds has seen both appreciation and depreciation.

We can plan all we want, but if we lay up for ourselves treasure upon earth, we have no guarantee that it is going to hold—which is exactly what Jesus said, "Do not store up for yourselves treasures on earth, where moth and rust destroy, and where thieves break in and steal" (Matthew 6:19).

You cannot guarantee that an investment today, no matter how safe it seems, is going to be there tomorrow. But Jesus gives us an alternative. "But store up for yourselves treasures in heaven, where moth and rust do not destroy, and where thieves do not break in and steal" (v. 20).

When I bring someone along in the kingdom, that

transaction is forever. When I yield myself to the living Christ and serve Him, the results are forever. When I worship Him, that praise doesn't end. These are investments that cannot be stolen and will not depreciate.

But I will not bring another along to trusting faith in Christ, I will not worship, I will not witness, unless my heart is there. For Jesus said, "Where your treasure is, there your heart will be also" (v. 21). If my treasure is based on the things of God, that treasure will remain and increase. If my treasure is in what rust and moths and thieves are going to destroy or take, I'm going to end up empty-handed. I can come full to the kingdom or I can come empty to the kingdom; the choice is mine. But if I come with hands full, that treasure will be there for others as well.

One great treasure we can leave behind is the certainty that we are safely, securely, and happily at home with God. For friends and family to know that is a comfort. They want to know that we are enjoying peace with God five years after our death, because we had peace with Him while we were still alive.

It's always good when we get things straight, and the psalmist helps us get things straight about death. In Psalm 88:10-12 he asks some questions of God. "Do you show your wonders to the dead?" Some people would say, "Oh, yes, God will forgive the dead, bless the dead." The answer is no. He asks another question. "Do those who are dead rise up and praise you?" "Oh, yes," some people say, "if their good works outweigh their bad." God's answer in Scripture is no. "Are your wonders known in the place of darkness?" The answer is no.

How do we know that? Scripture clearly teaches about death and life. First John 5:12 tells us, "He who has the Son has life; he who does not have the Son of God does not have life." Either we have life or we don't. And what we have now we carry with us into eternity. Eternal life or eternal death. Either way, we have it now. The question is never, "What will happen after death?" That is already decided right now by where we stand with the One who offers life. "He who has the Son has life." There is only one question—Do I have the Son or do I not have the Son? Jesus Christ is "the way and the truth and the life." No one comes to the Father except through Him (John 14:6). Those are God's words and we can live by them now and forever.

The Only One Left

Five years after your death, what witness will you have? It may be much greater than you think.

One morning in a church service an elderly man confessed that he wanted at last to place his trust in Jesus Christ as his Savior and Lord. Another elderly man in the congregation stood to his feet and in a voice quivering with emotion said, "For more than fifty years a group of men prayed for this friend. Those men have all gone home to heaven; I am the only one left to see God's answer to our prayers."

Those men had all witnessed to this man, had all prayed for him, had all had a part in giving a scriptural admonition. The Holy Spirit had used them in their younger years as they cared for this one who now, at last, yielded his soul to God. Those other men were gone, but they were remembered. Surely the man who made his confession of faith that day remembered and helped others remember as well.

A spiritual heritage stayed behind long after the men in that prayer group had grown old and died. They did not know that God would answer their prayers. They trusted, they believed, but they did not know. That day in church others learned of their faithfulness. The lesson about perseverance, faithfulness, and trusting God that those men who were long gone taught that Sunday in church was not soon forgotten. How many young men and women, boys and girls, learned that day that what we do in life carries on long after we're gone?

Men and women who rejected Christ while their parents lived have been known to come to faith years later, after their parents were dead. Slowly it dawned on them, through the quiet voice of the Holy Spirit, that they were rebelling against God. They realized that they were not rebelling against their parents or their parents' faith, even though their antagonism toward God may have started that way.

Think of a teenager rebelling against his parents. Soon it becomes more than rebellion; it continues, it feeds on itself into his twenties and thirties and forties so that he no longer can distinguish his youthful rebellion from the way he thinks about his parents and about God.

But now his parents are gone, and slowly he recalls positive thoughts, comments, and experiences. They break in, those remembrances, at odd moments, reflective moments, now no longer negative but positive. The focus of rebellion is gone, the pressure is off. He can be honest with himself—perhaps for the first time—and honest with God. He begins to realize, "I'm responsible for where I am. I'm not just a son or daughter anymore; I'm the older generation. What is really important to me? What really matters in my life? The ideas I fought against—that's really what it was, a fighting *against*, not *for*. The goals, the ideas, the plans I thought were important are really not so significant to me now." And many years after they have stood at a parent's graveside, rebellious sons or daughters have placed their own personal faith in the Savior.

And grandchildren, years after grandparents have gone, often begin to ask: "Why did Grandpa believe that? Why did Grandma quote the Bible so much?" The longing for their roots causes them in their own reflective moments to think again of what they had not seriously considered before. We can't limit the convicting work of the Holy Spirit of God to our own brief lifetime. A word spoken, a moment of prayer, a kind deed performed, like seeds sown, may come to fruition long after our own season of life has ended.

Planting What You May Never See

We read stories of ancient seeds, found in glaciers or even in sealed jars hidden away in caves, being planted and growing years later. How does it happen? We don't understand that miracle. It is God's mystery. God also knows how a human life is prepared to at last bring forth fruit from seed that was planted years before. I think it was Martin Luther who, when asked what he would do if he had only one day to live, replied, "I would plant a tree." Are you planting spiritual trees now, even though you may never see those trees come of age and bear fruit themselves?

We celebrate the conversion and missionary work of the Apostle Paul, but we don't always remember that Paul was once a hater of Christians, a persecutor who dragged them from their houses and put them in prison. We forget that he stood in the cheering section when Stephen was stoned to death. But Paul saw Stephen die and he heard his words. Someone may watch you die and at your death say, "She had what I want."

What legacy will you leave? "I have no legacy," you say, but that's not true, for God has given you a great legacy of words spoken, thoughts expressed, circumstances that He will bring back to someone's mind again and again as He points out to them the spiritual reason for your life.

Five years after your death, will somebody sing a hymn at church or hear one sung on the radio or at the funeral of another friend, and recall that long ago that hymn was your favorite? And will they then reflect, perhaps for the first time, on the words of that hymn— words that point to the Savior?

Whether yours is a funeral service, a simple graveside rite, or a memorial service, be sure that it is planned to point to the living Lord Christ. Five years after your death, people will recall your funeral.

Some people want a full funeral and have expressed that to relatives, so that others can come and see their remains in the casket. There is therapy in that, a feeling of finality. If this is your desire, be sure people understand that you are not really there. When someone says, "Oh, doesn't he look natural?" or "She looks like she is sleeping," make sure that someone will express your conviction that there is a difference between a body and a soul. Five years after your death some will reflect on that.

Let the pastor or person who leads your funeral service use hymns you have chosen to express great victory through faith in Christ. Let the Scriptures point to eternal life, a life that you experienced many years before you died and now know firsthand in all its fullness. Let those who speak about your life point to the One who gave you life. You are celebrating; help others to celebrate as well. Five years later, those who spoke and those who listened will recall.

For some people, your funeral will be their only time in a religious setting. Make it Gospel-centered, for these people are facing not just your homegoing but their own mortality. Behind stony faces some are thinking, "Am I prepared to die?" Help them to become ready for death by pointing to the One who offers them life. They may not connect it all in their thinking then, but five years later . . . maybe they will.

Resurrection—It's More Than a Belief

We have all heard the teaching, "Christ is risen if He has risen for you. The resurrection is real if it is real for you." That's just another way of saying, "It isn't real, but if you think it's real and it helps you, fine."

Well, the Apostle Paul answers that heresy, "If the dead are not raised, then Christ has not been raised either. And if Christ has not been raised, your faith is futile; you are still in your sins. . . . But Christ has indeed been raised from the dead" (1 Corinthians 15:16-17, 20).

Will your funeral lovingly confront and convict others with, "You are still in your sins. You're not forgiven"? That may be your most pointed and clear witness to some who never listened before. The apostle Paul summarizes, "If only for this life we have hope in Christ, we are to be pitied more than all men" (v. 19). And those standing by your casket or graveside without Christ are to be pitied, for they are wrong now and they will be wrong forever unless they accept Jesus' resurrection as a true and historical event.

Some at your funeral or five years later will understand at last what salvation is, that the resurrection is true. And how wonderful it will be when they come by faith to the risen Christ and receive new life. This could happen because of your funeral.

Suddenly It Clicks into Place

Lydia was a businesswoman who dealt in purple fabrics and rare dye. Scripture says that as she was listening to the Apostle Paul, "The Lord opened her heart to respond to Paul's message" (Acts 16:14). Just like that, her heart was opened and she was ready.

That's the way it is for many. Suddenly the Gospel clicks into place and it is so logical and clear. Suddenly people say, "Oh, that's why Jesus died for me," or, "Now I understand what it means to know God in a personal way." And it becomes so clear that with enthusiasm they rejoice, "Yes, I can see it now."

Perhaps you do not want a traditional funeral. Perhaps you have chosen cremation so that the costs are minimal and preparations less, knowing full well that you are absent from the body and present with the Lord. Perhaps you are having a simple graveside service. The message can still be the same. "Jesus reigns." You are experiencing now the fullness of the eternal life that you experienced only in part during your days on earth. You have made Jesus' resurrection central—and people will remember.

It may be that you prefer a memorial time when people remember your walk with Christ. Perhaps there will be somebody present at that gathering, in a church or home or restaurant, who will testify that you are the person who brought them along to faith or helped them grow in Christ. If you have relatives who live at a distance, perhaps you can suggest in your funeral preparations that they not come to the place where you lived but stay in their own community, gather friends or relatives who knew you, and have a memorial service there. Let them come together some evening or Sunday afternoon and make it a time of worship and praise to God. For some who are there, the recollection will trigger understanding as, suddenly, the Good News clicks into place.

May you leave a legacy that others can recall. Let them recall it. It will give them a great sense of who God is and what He has done.

Five years after your death, if you have a burial place, people will come to look and remember. They may even be strangers who stop on their way to a nearby grave. If you have a grave stone, let it indicate your trust in the risen Christ with a portion of Scripture or a word about being alive in Christ etched in stone. Between the dates of birth and death, let there be something that captures what God did in your life. Someday, when people walk by, years or generations later, they may glance at that stone and be reminded again that God reigns, that here are the remains of one who believed in Christ.

When people stand at your grave, you will be in another city, whose builder and maker is God. You will be in the holy place with the One who is life and light. Behind you will be the legacy of your life. Five years later—maybe even longer—your legacy will make the meaning of eternal life click into place for someone.

Joshua left a legacy, and it had nothing to do with himself, but everything to do with God. In Joshua 23:14 we read, "Now I am about to go the way of all the earth." In other words, I'm going to die. "You know with all your heart and soul that not one of all the good promises the Lord your God gave you has failed."

Think of it. Joshua had lived a long life and fought some hard battles. And he knew that not one thing the Lord had promised had failed. Not one part of God's Word had he found to be untrue or unfulfilled. We too have found that not one thing the Lord promised has failed. And when we have gone to heaven, we'll have proven to those left behind, "You can trust God. He will not fail you. He never failed me." When people look back at your life they will be able to say, "That's right; God never did."

When God Makes It Happen

When we leave this world, we will have entered a new order. In Revelation 21:4 we read, "He will wipe every tear from their eyes. There will be no more death or mourning or crying or pain, for the old order of things has passed away." It will happen for us when God makes it happen. And when He does, there will be no more tears for us, no more death for us, no more mourning. There will be no more crying, and no more pain, because all that belongs to the old order, and for us the old order has passed away.

We can make sure that after we're gone others will experience Revelation 21:4, because we were here for them before we moved to heaven. Someday we'll meet them again and have a wonderful reunion, rejoicing as tears are wiped away. And we will worship God together.

Many of you are blessed with believing families, children, grandchildren, and extended family—all members of the family of Christ, all walking with the Savior, loving Him, serving Him faithfully. Five years after you're gone there will be many times of recollection.

"Remember when?" they will say. And your name will be mentioned along with a remembrance of a service performed, an act of kindness, a lesson taught.

They will relive something you said or did and it will encourage and strengthen them. "I remember what Dad did when he faced this situation," someone will say. And they will pattern their decision after your example. "I remember when Mother . . ." and they will describe it, and that will be enough to give hope or comfort or guidance.

The Christian heritage you leave behind will encourage people in other families too, for many generations, as your story is told.

One Small Act

A few years ago in *Decision* magazine we published an article by Richard Bewes, rector of All Souls, Langham Place, London. We asked him to tell us of his heritage. It goes back to Tuesday evening, September 26, 1882, when a servant in the Bewes' house took fourteen-year-old Tommy Bewes to hear evangelist D.L. Moody. Young Tommy met the Savior that evening.

Tommy Bewes later became an evangelical Anglican clergyman. His oldest son Cecil went into full-time ministry and missionary service in Africa. Of Cecil Bewes's four children, one is a missionary surgeon; one, a Christian businessman, is involved in Scripture Union; a sister married a clergyman; and Richard is a clergyman. Richard Bewes said, "My dad once remarked, 'I've just been going through my Christmas list—for family alone. How many names do you think I had on it? One hundred and two.' The wonderful thing is that we all seem to be involved in Christian activities."[1]

Even when we are limited with not much to offer—an ordinary life, we say—we find it isn't ordinary at all. That household servant who took Tommy Bewes to that meeting did something extraordinary. The results of that one act may reach millions.

We may not think we have accomplished memorable things in our lives, but we may have encouraged someone even when we didn't know it. We may have taught even when we weren't aware of it. We may have been a blessing even when we didn't realize it. We may have hugged a child, offered guidance, given hope. We show, we teach, and we help others to say, "I can live that way too."

When we follow Christians who have gone before, we have a running start in the wonderful race that the Apostle Paul speaks of. We have the advantage of a biblical heritage, the teaching, the experiences of Christian mentors to build on. That was our privilege when we were younger and that's the privilege now of others who come along after us.

God Won't Waste Our Legacy

We live in a time when families are seen to be very special, and people are withdrawing to be in their own cocoon with their own family. Family is important, and that importance reaches back to years before. Younger people want to know about grandparents and parents, and they want to leave a legacy for their own children as well.

We are givers of a legacy. The excitement we have, the stories we tell, the events we recall, and the miracles of God in our lives should not be lost at our death. We have lived with spiritual hope; we die with spiritual hope. That is our legacy, and God will not waste that legacy. Long after we're gone God will use it.

We plant seeds, knowing that the plants will come up, because there is a Master Gardener who is watching and tending the garden. There will be a harvest and it will be His. We plant in lives, we give our treasures, we invest words and love; they all will bring fruit.

We are an offering; our lives are a gift. First we give to God, then to others. During our younger years, with the struggles of work and raising a family and the worries that go with a busy life, perhaps with less than enough money to get by, we may not have thought so much about the offering of who we are. But in our later years, when we have more time for reflection, we understand what God has given to us, the valuable things, and the gifts we have to offer.

This is our time to give. These last years are our best years. An old English proverb says, "The older the fiddle, the sweeter the tune." As we play that tune now, we know it will be heard and remembered.

Dwight L. Moody once spoke of what was ahead for him. He said, "Someday you will read in the papers that D.L. Moody of East Northfield is dead. Don't you believe a word of it. At that moment I shall be more alive than now. I shall have gone up higher, that is all."

Years after you've gone up higher, who will be saying in a reflective moment, "I will never forget..."? Five years after you're gone perhaps someone will say to another, "Let me tell you about...."

The story told will be about you!

For Reflection:

1. Imagine what people will remember about you five years after you're gone. Are there memories you still want to add?

2. Five years after your funeral, what do you want people to recall and reflect on—a hymn, a Scripture? Are you making sure that they will have that memory?

3. Are there special people you are praying about now, trusting God that even after you're gone the meaning of the Good News will click into place?

4. Are you asking God to let you show how a Christian dies? That may be one of your greatest teachings.

5. If you knew for sure that you would die tomorrow, what would you be doing today?

Finally: Have you thought about friends who are missing out on their best years? Will you tell them what you are going to do with your remaining years? Will you let them read your copy of this book or give them a copy of their own so that they too will begin their own "best years"?

Endnotes

Chapter One

1. Nolan Zavoral, "Ninety-nine and Kind of a Ham," Minneapolis *Star Tribune,* 19 August 1993.
2. James H. Kraakevik and Dotsey Welliver, editors. *Partners in the Gospel,* a BGC monograph, copyright Billy Graham Center, Wheaton College, Wheaton, Illinois. N.D., 21.

Chapter Two

1. Billy Strachan, *You Can Be Fruitful in Your Isolation* (Bromley, Kent, England: OM Publishing, 1991), 24, 29, 41, 69, 93.

Chapter Three

1. Gilbert Brin, "Ambition: How to Manage Success and Failure," *Psychology Today,* September/October 1992, 48.

Chapter Four

1. Bill Waldrop, "From the Executive Director," *Networker*, January/February 1994, 4.

2. Russell Chandler, *Racing Toward 2001* (San Francisco: Harper and Row, 1992), 57.

Chapter Five

1. William H. Willimon, "Reaching and Teaching the Abandoned Generation," *Christian Century*, 20 October 1993, 1016–19.

Chapter Seven

1. Thomas Moore, "Care of the Soul: the benefits—and costs—of a more spiritual life," *Psychology Today*, May/June 1993, 28.

Chapter Eight

1. Roz Hutchinson, "Retirement Gives Couple Time to Help Others During Disasters," Wichita *Eagle*, 18 November 1993.

2. Sharon Sheehan, "Why Sex Ed Is Failing Our Kids," *Christianity Today*, 5 October 1992, 37.

3. Robert Franklin, "In a Scary Place, an Angel of Kindness," Minneapolis *Star Tribune*, 26 December 1993.

Chapter Nine

1. Henry Ward Beecher, The Optimists' Good Morning (Boston: Little Brown & Company, 1907), 192.

Chapter Ten

1. *The Quotable Lewis*, 245, *Letters of C.S. Lewis*, 21 December 1941, 197. Taken from a calendar.

Chapter Eleven

1. *The Quotable Lewis*, 807, *Letters of C.S. Lewis*, 17 July 1953, 250. Taken from a calendar.

Chapter Twelve

1. Richard Bewes, "Three Generations: The Testimony of a Family," *Decision*, September 1982, 3.